GOD'S
PRAYER
PROGRAM

T. M. Moore is a Fellow of the Wilberforce Forum and Pastor of Teaching Ministries at Cedar Springs Presbyterian Church in Knoxville, Tennessee. His essays, reviews, articles, and poetry have appeared in a wide range of journals, and he is the author of 10 books, including *Preparing the Church for Revival* ISBN 1-85792-698-6 and *A Mighty Fortress* ISBN 1-85792-868-7. He and his wife, Susie, have four children and ten grandchildren, and make their home in Concord, TN.

GOD'S PRAYER PROGRAM

Passionately Using the Psalms in Prayer

T. M. Moore

CHRISTIAN FOCUS

Permission for the use of the schedules that appear in Appendix 1 is granted from Baker Book House, for material from T. M. Moore, *The Psalms for Prayer* (Grand Rapids: Baker Books, 2002, a division of Baker Book House Company), pp. 312-316.

ISBN 1-84550-061-X

10 9 8 7 6 5 4 3 2 1

Published in 2005
by
Christian Focus Publications, Ltd.,
Geanies House, Fearn, Tain,
Ross-shire, IV20 1TW, Scotland.

www.christianfocus.com

Printed and bound by
Norhaven, Denmark

Cover Design by Alister MacInnes

Contents

For Steven Wright

THE PSALTER SAIL

*"Fear not," said he, "for we have our God Himself as our guide and
helper. And ship your oars and set the sail; and God will guide His
own boat and company as He pleases."*

Brendan of Clonfert (ca. AD 560)[1]

His heart's eye firmly set upon a land
of promised blessing, Brendan led his troop
of sixteen faithful friends to build a sloop
of skins, that they might follow where the hand
of God would lead. Full hard they rowed against
the unknown sea, yet they could not prevail.
So Brendan shipped the oars and raised the sail,
and let the wind of God propel him thence.

As Brendan found their feeble frames unfit
to gain the blessing, and unfurled his sail
to catch the welcome winds of God, so we
who seek the Savior's face in prayer must quit
mere fleshly schemes, and principally avail
us of the psalter sail to cross this sea.

---

[1] Robert Van de Meyer, *Celtic Fire* (New York: Doubleday, 1990),
p. 45; Charles Plummer, ed. and tr., *Lives of Irish Saints* (Oxford: Oxford University Press, 1922 [1997]), p. 53.

INTRODUCTION:

A MIGHTY STRUGGLE

The best thing, when it is possible, is to keep the patient from the serious intention of praying altogether.

-Screwtape to Wormwood[1]

"For we do not know what to pray as we ought..."[2]

I don't recall the first time I ever came across this bit of apostolic insight; I must have read that passage many times during those early years of my walk with the Lord. But I do remember my frequent and frustrated response to it: You got that right!

Some believers, no doubt, have never had to struggle with prayer. I am not one of those, and I suspect that my experience of laboring to arrive at some satisfactory practice of the discipline of prayer mirrors what most have known who have ever taken up the challenge of this discipline.

For the first twenty years of my life as a believer I approached the discipline of prayer from many different angles. Using a variety of practices and props, I struggled with all my might, like Brendan and his sixth-century crew of missionary monks, to row my way to the blessings of God. But much of the time I felt I was making little headway. That prayer is important, and that all Christians should make prayer a vital part of their walk with the Lord, was drummed into me from the first days of my life in Christ by those who helped me begin to grow in grace. But that making effective use of the discipline of prayer can be a mighty struggle, one that can disappoint as often as it satisfies, well, somehow I failed to pay attention when they mentioned that.

I was taught to pray at first using the familiar "ACTS" formula. Some time in each of my prayers, I was told, should be given to Adoring the Lord, some to Confessing my sins, some to giving Him Thanks, and some to Supplications, or, prayers for my needs and those of others. Dutifully, I set out to master the use of this simple and helpful formula. For a while in those early years this proved to be a very satisfactory approach to prayer. But then I began to have questions.

For example, were my attempts at adoring the Lord the kinds of expressions of love that He wanted to hear? Was I saying them correctly? Adoring Him for the right things? The right reasons? Adoring Him as much as I should? With as much sincerity as He desired? Conversely, was I failing to adore Him in any ways I should due to ignorance, neglect, or other reason? Was I even saying as much as I wanted to say in my expressions of love for the God Who had saved me and was filling my life with so many blessings?

What about my prayers of confession? Were they sincere? Were my motives what they ought to have been? Was I covering all the bases, confessing everything I should? As often as I should? Confessing with the right attitude? Was I even using words that

God would find acceptable? Was it all right to confess sins I didn't even know about, or should I just let those sleeping dogs lie?

Once the questions began, they quickly spilled over into every area of my prayers: Was I as thankful as I should be? For as much as I should? What was I leaving out? Should I be thanking God with greater frequency? Greater fervency? Greater breadth? Was I failing to give thanks for anything? Should I give thanks even when I don't feel thankful? If so, how do I do that?

The questions ranged even farther in the area of supplications: Whom was I leaving out? What was I failing to mention? Was I asking amiss, for things I wanted rather than things God wanted me to have? Are all the things my friends asked me to pray about even legitimate in the eyes of the Lord? Was I forgetting anything I had promised to pray for? What about the missionaries? Should I be praying for them? What about the lost? The leaders of my church? The rulers of the world's nations? My neighbor next door? What should I be praying about for all these people? How could I ever remember all this anyway?

Such questions led to frustration and disappointment with prayer the way I was then pursuing it. And these were the easy questions! The harder ones were the more personal questions relating to my attitudes and conduct in prayer: What does God think when my mind drifts like it does so often? Am I taking enough time in prayer?

Saying things the right way, with the right attitude of heart? Should I pray things I've promised to pray even if I don't feel right doing so? Should I be kneeling, praying to myself, praying out loud, raising my hands? Does God care that I don't say "Thee" and "shouldst"? Should I be saying them? When should I pray? And how often? Does God know how frustrating and unsatisfying I find this whole business of prayer? Does He know that I'm ready to give it up? Does He care? Is He angry with me? Does He know that sometimes this business of prayer makes me a little angry at Him?

I knew there had to be more to prayer than what I was experiencing. Nevertheless, before long I began to be so burdened by these and a hundred other questions and concerns that I found it easier not to pray than to pray. Yet I knew that was wrong. So I took to praying spontaneously, praying as I "felt led of the Spirit" to pray. I abandoned the regular discipline of prayer and just sort of waited on the Lord throughout the day to call me to pray for this or that. If I felt the Spirit leading me to pray in the morning, then I would pray for as long as I felt His leading. I followed the same general regimen at other times during the day.

At first, this was a liberating experience. When I did take the time to pray, I felt some assurance that God had called me to it and was therefore listening to me. I tried to let my words be as spontaneous and sincere as I knew how to make them, and I allowed my mind to range in whatever directions I felt the

Spirit was leading me to consider. I felt refreshed and satisfied in my prayers. That is, when I prayed.

Before long, however, I realized that I was praying less than ever. I'm certain that He must have been calling me, given the fact, for example, that He commands us to pray without ceasing. Either I was not listening or was so spiritually dull or otherwise distracted that I could not hear Him calling. Whatever it was, I found that I was praying very little during the course of the day, and the times I did respond to the Lord and pray were becoming shorter and shorter. Now I had reams of unanswered questions, a growing burden of guilt, and no effective way of dealing with either of these in prayer.

I next tried various prayer lists, always with the same result. They satisfied my need to talk to God for a while, but they failed to answer my questions or bring any relief to my frustration with prayer. In fact, my numerous prayer lists simply created even more questions, like, Do I have as many lists as I should? Am I really sincere about what I'm praying with respect to these lists? Worse, getting through my various lists in prayer began to be what the Protestant reformers used to accuse their Catholic opponents of – *opera operata*, mere religious duties that I performed in the belief that just performing them was all that God required.[3] Somehow, I guessed – I hoped – that praying through those lists would work whether or not I felt or meant my prayers.

That, however, did not bring the sense of fulfillment in prayer that I was seeking. I tried writing my own prayers. Useless. I tried compiling and using the prayers of others. No good. I even tried just letting the Lord's prayer (Matthew 6:9-13) be my only guide, but not even that helped, since I still had all the unanswered questions concerning the various categories of prayer suggested by that masterpiece. I knew I was supposed to pray "this way," but I had almost no words, or, at best, very unsatisfying words, with which to fill up the areas of prayer our Lord indicated in His model prayer. Here the Lord Himself had gone to the trouble of giving me a guide to prayer, and I wasn't even able to follow those simple instructions!

I could not figure it out. God wanted me to pray, and I knew I should pray. I wanted to pray, but I was getting nowhere. I felt as though I was beginning to hate prayer, for it had become a burden too great for me to bear. I had been promised that God had a wonderful plan for my life, but I wasn't finding this part of it so wonderful. I had been pulling at the oars of prayer with all my might, and I wasn't making much headway in my spiritual journey. However, I knew I had to find a way to gain victory in this struggle with prayer.

Had it been current at the time, I'm sure I would have felt like Jack Nicholson in the film, *As Good As It Gets*, when, in the depth of his frustration, he walks out of his psychiatrist's office and says to all the waiting patients, "Do you ever wonder if this is as good as it gets?"

Had I some Elisha to draw back the curtains of my spiritual blindness,[4] I might have seen the demons roaring with laughter at my hapless condition. I was a failure in prayer, and I concluded that Paul was right, I did not know how to pray as I ought. But I took no comfort in that apostolic insight.

Somewhere along the line in this growing struggle I began to notice something in my reading of Scripture and Church history. I observed that many of the great saints of the past fell easily and often to quoting the psalms and other passages of Scripture in their prayers. In fact, they seemed to rely on Scripture so frequently in their prayers that I began to wonder if they were either just unimaginative or lazy in prayer, or if they simply didn't know any better. Here were these great soldiers of the cross, to whom I was looking for guidance in my faith, and in the matter of prayer, and they seemed hopelessly stuck in the words of the psalms and other parts of the Bible. Didn't these people know how to pray as they should?

That was the key for me. *Of course* they did not know how to pray as they should, any more than I – or you – do. The difference between them and me was that they had acknowledged the fact, had given up the pretense of depending on their own devices or schemes, and were finding satisfaction, blessing, and great power to serve the Lord in prayer by letting God's prayer program guide and sustain them. They had shipped the oars of their own efforts in prayer and hoisted the sail of God's prayer guide to carry them along in this most important discipline, and the Spirit of God filled that sail so that they mightily prevailed before the throne of grace. Their prayers were filled with quotes from the psalms, addresses to God that I recognized from that great song book of Scripture, and simple phrases, formulas, and ideas lifted from the psalms and inserted into their prayers at just the appropriate place to give their prayers real beauty and power. I concluded that the psalms came so easily and so often to them in their written prayers because they must have been using those God-given prayers in a disciplined way at other times of prayer as well. Like an athlete, who in the midst of a game or match, makes a certain move or executes a particular skill, virtually without thinking, because he has practiced it over and over during the week, these great saints fell into praying the psalms in public prayers because they used them so frequently in their personal times with the Lord.

I began to try praying portions of Scripture myself, especially from the psalms. At first it was awkward and seemed extremely artificial. I felt like a little child playing at prayer, merely imitating what I'd heard someone else doing in prayer without really understanding what I was saying or why. But this is how children learn, and something deep inside me said that it was worth staying the course. Not that I was determined to become some kind of exclusive psalm-prayer, that is, that my prayers would only ever be in the words of the psalms. But I believed that developing the discipline of using the psalms as a guide to my prayers at certain times of the day would not only provide a reliable regimen of prayer that I could regularly practice and improve, but also would strengthen my prayers at other times, giving me not only the precise words to use when I needed them, but also supplying guidelines to prayer and assurance that the words I used would be pleasing to God and, therefore, more likely to gain a favorable hearing.

For several years I pursued this discipline of praying through some of the psalms, mainly those with which I was familiar and felt comfortable– 8, 19, 23, and so forth. At the same time, I returned to various of the practices I had previously tried in order to bring some balance and fullness to my prayers. But I found that nothing satisfied in prayer quite so much as simply letting a psalm guide me. Increasingly, I found that the psalms provided me with the words I needed; they led my mind to recall the requests others had asked me to remember; and they tapped the wellsprings of affection in my heart so that I could feel in prayer what God wanted me to. I began to discover a new joy in prayer, together with a confidence and assurance I had never known in prayer before. I began to find in prayer a greater sense of the presence of God, and a deeper sense of wonder and mystery at being before the throne of grace. I actually started to look forward to prayer. I began to schedule more time for prayer into my day. I also noticed that at times when I was praying outside the context of my personal prayers – in Bible studies, over meals, with friends, in leading worship – that phrases, quotes, and ideas from the psalms began to find their way into my words. The discipline of praying the psalms regularly was beginning to inform and strengthen all my prayers, just as I believe it must have done for the great saints of the Church throughout the ages, and I was starting to realize something more of the promise of prayer that Scripture holds out for us.

In due course I began to pray using all the psalms, working my way through the entire psalter on a regular basis. As I did, I found more satisfaction, more power, more assurance, more wonder, and more joy and peace in my prayers than I had ever known before. To be sure, this was no new discovery on my part. Great saints of the past had been down this path many times before, as we shall see. But it was new to me. And it was truly exciting! At the same time, I was praying more than I ever had before, and more frequently, and I have never noticed that my work has suffered or that I'm missing something I'd rather do because I've spent too much time in prayer. And I began to see more answers to my prayers as I kept going back over the prayer list God Himself had provided. They were not necessarily the answers I had sought, but I could clearly see that God was answering prayers according to His purposes and will for my life. He was hearing me when I prayed, and I could see in the answers He provided that He was shaping and growing me through prayer as well.

In short, I began to know the presence of God's Spirit, filling the sails of my prayers with His powerful presence, as He helped me, through the psalms, to realize the promise of prayer more and more.

This book is an attempt to share what I have learned about praying the psalms – following God's prayer program – as a foundation for our prayers: how we can do this, why we should, and what we can expect if we do. My focus is on the discipline of praying the psalms as the basis for all our other prayers. I do not claim to have mastered this discipline, nor have all my questions and concerns regarding the practice of prayer gone away. Neither do I wish to suggest that all our prayers must be from the psalms alone. But, because of what I have experienced praying the psalms, using the psalms as my basic prayer program, prayer has become for me such a wonderful haven of sweet fellowship with the Lord and of confident conversation with Him, that I want to share what I have learned with anyone who may be struggling with this important discipline as I did. And the responses of students whom I have taught to pray using the psalms, and of those who have used my compilation, *The Psalms for Prayer*,[5] lead me to believe that others might be able to find help in their prayers by adopting God's prayer program, the psalms, as their fundamental practice of this important discipline.

In the pages that follow we will look, first, at why prayer is important. Unless we are first convinced of the importance of the discipline of prayer to our life in Christ, we will not be much motivated to learn how to pray as we ought. Once we understand the important place of prayer in the life of faith, and all that God promises through this discipline, we will want to take it up eagerly, and according to God's purpose and design.

Next we will take a brief look at the psalms and the way they have been used in worship and prayer by the people of God from all ages. We are part of a grand tradition of the followers of Christ, and we must be willing to learn from and carry on that tradition, not only in what we should believe, but also in how we practice our faith through such disciplines as prayer. Previous generations of the followers of Christ found the psalms a valuable resource for their prayers. As we are the beneficiaries of their faithfulness in many ways, we should be willing to learn from them in this area as well.

Then we shall examine some of the different approaches to praying the psalms – using God's prayer list – that I have found helpful. My purpose in this section will be to equip the reader with a variety of ways to pray through the psalms, letting God's Spirit lead and fill us as we unfurl the psalter sail that God has graciously provided for our journey of faith. This will help you to appreciate the great flexibility, diversity, range, and power of the psalms, as well as to experience the deep satisfaction that praying them can bring.

After this we will consider some general guidelines and special challenges that come to us as we take up God's prayer program and use the psalms as the basis for our prayers. How do we appropriate all the references to Israel, Jerusalem, and the enemies of God's people? What use can we make of the various imprecatory psalms? What about when a psalm just doesn't express what I'm going through, or when it expresses something that I'm not experiencing?

Next, we will look at the promise of God's prayer program. How should we expect to benefit from using the psalms in prayer? What will the Lord do in my life if I stay the course with Him in this discipline? How will I be changed?

Finally, we will consider the greatest challenge in praying the psalms – that of staying with the program in the face of temptations to give it up. Following God's prayer program is not an easy business. It can be difficult and frustrating at times, and we may feel like moving on to something else, going back to some of those old devices and schemes we've tried before, or maybe finding some new ones, or even giving up on prayer altogether. How do we recognize and resist these temptations so that we can continue to know the power of prayer God's prayer program can provide?

Three appendices will conclude our study. In the first I will provide three different schedules for praying through the entire psalter on a regular basis. Readers should find one or more of these helpful in beginning to submit to this discipline. The second will include some samples of psalms set to familiar hymn tunes for singing. Singing the psalms, as we shall see, can be a valuable addition to one's times of prayer. Many – if not all – of the psalms were meant to be sung; while we have lost the original melodies that were written for them, we may create "new songs" of our own, using familiar tunes to allow us to sing the psalms of God to the praise of the glory of His grace. The final appendix is really more of an index, suggesting psalms to pray for selected topics, needs, or concerns. Readers may find this index helpful in getting started with God's prayer program.

My overall objective in this study is to help you see that the psalms are, like Brendan's sail, a wonderfully useful tool for catching the wind of God's Spirit as He comes to us on the sea of our lives and carries us along in His power. We cannot get to where God is taking us by our own efforts. We need the power of His Spirit, carrying us along on the course marked out by His Word. God's prayer program is, like Brendan's sail, the means of gathering the Spirit's power to propel us on our journey, for the prayers God has provided us are the most reliable aids to which we can turn. By learning to pray the psalms – by using God's prayer program, not instead of, but as the foundation for all our other approaches to prayer – we can enjoy a more consistent, more powerful, and more meaningful, and more truly satisfying experience of prayer than we have ever known before.

I want to thank Willie MacKenzie, Ian Thompson, and all the good folk at Christian Focus Publications for taking on this project. Willie's own example of praying the psalms, and the encouragement he gave me over breakfast one morning, rekindled my belief in this project and my hope that many might find it useful. And, of course, I am grateful to my wife, Susie, for her encouragement and many, many helpful suggestions in helping to prepare this book for publication. Her editorial and other suggestions have been, as always, invaluable. This book goes forth with the prayer that God will use it to help rekindle joy and power in prayer in many of His people, to the greater praise of the glory of His grace.

T. M. Moore

Concord, TN
Spring, 2004

---

[1] C. S. Lewis, *The Screwtape Letters* (New York: Simon and Schuster, 1961), p. 28.

[2] Romans 8:26.

[3] For a good look at how the reformers viewed these practices, see Martin Luther's *The Pagan Servitude of the Church*. When I first read that tract, I felt as though he was looking into my own heart.

[4] 2 Kings 6:17.

[5] T. M. Moore, *The Psalms for Prayer* (Grand Rapids: Baker, 2002).

1.

THE NEED FOR A PROGRAM

In prayer lies not only our unity with God, but also the unity of our personal life.

-Abraham Kuyper[1]

To You, O LORD, I call; my rock, be not deaf to me, lest, if you be silent to me, I become like those who go down to the pit.

- Psalm 28:1

Hear my prayer, Lord; I cry out out to You. Receive my prayer, open Your ears to me, Lord, and answer me. For if You do not hear and answer me, if I cannot meet with You in prayer, and be heard, and hear Your answers, then, Lord, I have no more hope than an unbeliever.

My friend had just finished pouring out his heart to me about the sorry state of his marriage. He was willing to take most of the blame for the situation, but he felt his wife had some responsibility as well. He had tried to be nicer, more attentive and more thoughtful, and less wrapped up in himself, but it just didn't seem to work. Either his wife didn't appreciate the efforts he was making, or he was not able to sustain them for very long. At any rate, they always ended up at the same place – angry, quarreling, threatening, and spending the night alone. He was at the end of his rope.

I asked him if he'd prayed about his situation, to which he replied, "Yeah, well, at the beginning I did.

But it didn't seem to do any good, so I haven't lately. I don't much feel like praying, and I don't really have the time for it. Besides, why should God listen to me after the way I've treated my wife? And why, with all the really important things He has to do, should He even care about what's happening in my home? I don't even know what to pray for anymore."

In that response are six of the most common excuses people give for why they don't pray as they should. Did you catch them?

I tried it and it didn't work. Sometimes we can have little patience with God's timing. In our sitcom society we're so used to things working themselves out within the space of thirty minutes to an hour, that we think God should operate in the same manner. If I pray for something, God should respond within a reasonably short time. But when His timing fails to coincide with our expectations, we become disillusioned with prayer and give up appealing to Him, believing that prayer doesn't make any difference, at least not for us.

I don't feel like praying. We are of the generation that was raised believing, "If it feels good, do it!" And if it doesn't feel good, or it's just too much trouble, we won't exert ourselves. Our feelings, which are already weighing us down, defeat us from appealing to the very thing that can lift us above our feelings. And so we don't pray because we don't feel like it.

I don't have much time for prayer. Of course, we all have the same amount of time each day, and we tend to do in that time the things we consider to be truly important. It's not that we don't have time for prayer; it's that we do not see prayer as a priority for our time.

I'm not worthy. Sometimes we may feel that God won't listen to us because we're such schmucks. We think that only really holy and righteous people can get through to God. He's not going to listen to us until we get our act together and clean ourselves up. And, since we don't seem to be able to do that on our own, there's not much chance He'll be listening to us any time soon. So why even bother?

My concerns are so petty. After all, He has a universe to manage, a Kingdom to advance, a Church to build, lost souls to save, the prayers of great saints to honor, and on and on. Why should God consider the everyday problems of wretched folks like me? What makes me worthy of a place in His agenda? Why trouble Him with the small stuff when He's got bigger things to do?

I don't know what to pray. It's pretty hard to have a consistent prayer relationship with God if we're just sitting there, staring out into the void the whole time. Sometimes we don't pray as we should because we've found either that our prayers all sound alike, we've already prayed everything we know to pray, or we just don't know how to put our feelings and concerns into words.

Perhaps you've experienced one or more of these excuses for not praying. I certainly have, and continue to be tempted to fall back on one or more of them from time to time. It is easy enough for us to roll over and play dead with respect to prayer when the trials of everyday life are threatening to overwhelm us. Our natural inclination is not to pray anyway but simply to resolve to do better the next time, to fix things ourselves. Not praying comes easy to us. However, as Christ showed during His temptation,[2] the easy way is seldom the correct way in the life of faith.

Before we actually launch into the matter of using the psalms in prayer, it will be good for us to make sure that we actually believe in this discipline – really, and not just intellectually – and that we understand why it is important to pray. Consistent, meaningful, and satisfying prayer is a difficult discipline to master. Unless we are completely convinced of the absolute importance of prayer and of its role in the life of faith, we will always find that our approach to prayer is haphazard, tentative, shoddy, and unsatisfying.

I want to examine briefly seventeen reasons why we ought to pray. There are no doubt many more than that, but the seventeen we will look at in this chapter have provided sufficient motivation for me over the years to keep me working at this discipline through struggles, failures, and defeats, until now my times in prayer have become the most important part of my day. Be forewarned, however, that merely understanding these seventeen reasons to pray will not make you more consistent or give you more power in prayer. They will only give you sound reasons to pray. The rest is up to you, as you wait on the Lord and draw on His power in prayer. Happily, however, as we shall see, God Himself has established a program for prayer to help us in making the best use of this important discipline. And His Spirit waits to fill us with His presence and power in prayer as we take up the program God, in His mercy and grace, has prepared especially for us.

PRAYER IS THE MOST CHARACTERISTIC ASPECT OF THE LIFE OF FAITH[3]

We can say with confidence that prayer is the most characteristic attribute of true believers. It is the thing above all else that makes them stand out from others. We see this emphasis throughout the Word of God.

After the fall into sin and the murder of Abel by Cain, God was pleased to give Adam and Eve another son, whom Eve named Seth. After that, men began *to call upon the name of the Lord*.[4] What follows then is a listing of the first generation of those first believers, people who were characterized primarily by their practice of turning to God in prayer. Those who came to be known as the "sons of God" could be identified as such by their frequent use of prayer.

Abraham, with whom God entered into the covenant which is the privileged relationship that all true believers have with Him,[5] built altars unto the Lord as places to meet Him in prayer.[6] This was his first act upon arriving in the land to which God led him, and important turning-points in his life are marked by the mention of his erecting altars for prayer and worship. Later, Abraham seems to have had an accustomed place for coming before the Lord for those times of intimate spiritual conversation.[7]

Moses was also characterized by prayer. He met with God for extended periods of mutual interaction as God prepared him to lead His people out of captivity. Later, we find him conversing with God in prayer when he received the Law of God and on various occasions when he interceded for the people.

David knew that prayer was the place to turn to God for healing, protection from enemies, guidance in everyday affairs, and a host of other reasons.[8]

All the prophets and the great kings of Judah spent time with God in prayer, often, as we shall see, at several periods during the day.

Certainly the Lord Jesus knew the value of prayer, and that He needed to resort often to it in order to fulfill His earthly calling. The many uses He made of prayer hardly need citing: He often arose well before dawn to pray; stayed up all night long for prayer; prayed and fasted for extended periods of time; broke into spontaneous prayer in public places; frequently chose solitude in prayer over the busy-ness of ministry; and prayed intensely for Himself and His followers in the Garden and elsewhere.

The Apostle Paul tells us that perhaps the first conscious act of a true believer is to call out the name of God in prayer.[9] The true saints of God in the Book of Revelation offer up prayers to Him that are like sweet incense in His nostrils.[10]

There's just no way around it: Prayer is perhaps the single most identifying attribute of a true believer in God. Not that people in other religions do not pray; certainly they do. But it is all but impossible to describe the Christian life or to think of being in a relationship with the living God through faith in Jesus Christ without the discipline of prayer being a significant part of that experience. And, for this reason, we who love the Lord and desire to follow Him will want to learn how to pray as we should, and to adopt a program of prayer that will allow us to make maximum use and gain maximum benefit from this great privilege God extends to us.

GOD COMMANDS US TO PRAY

We can hardly expect to have much of a meaningful relationship with God, or to be of much usefulness in His Kingdom, if we fail to adhere to His most fundamental commands. If, for example, we refuse to call upon Him in prayer, as He requires:

> Offer to God a sacrifice of thanksgiving, and perform your vows to the Most High; and call upon me in the day of trouble; I will deliver you, and you shall glorify me.[11]

> Call to me and I will answer you, and will tell you great and hidden things that you have not known.[12]

31

> Ask, and it will be given to you; seek, and you shall find;
> knock, and it will be opened to you.[13]

What could be clearer or more plain? God commands His people to pray. God's people should respond eagerly and often to this command, and make prayer an important part of their lives. If we are slow to submit to this command, and to learn how to pray as we ought, how can we expect Him to bless us? How will we ever know the full and abundant life He promises if we're not willing to adhere to His requirements for attaining it? Many Christians wonder why their lives in Christ are so flat, unexciting, and unfulfilling. Look to their prayers. We may expect to find in many instances a direct correlation between the amount of time spent in prayer, and the quality of those prayers, and the amount of satisfaction and power believers know in their daily walk with Christ. God commands us to pray; therefore, let us learn how to do so in a way that will be pleasing to Him and fulfilling for us. And if He has provided a program of prayer to aid us in fulfilling this command, then by all means, let us hasten to apply ourselves to it.

PRAYER REMINDS US OF OUR NEED FOR GOD

Augustine noted that people are prone to depend upon themselves, to live their own lives in their own strength and according to their own ideas of what is right for them. They want to do it on their own, find their own way, figure it out all by themselves. He wrote, "This desire for sovereignty is a deadly corrosive to human spirits."[14] When we are on our knees before the Lord, turning over to Him all the matters that so befuddle and bemuse us, and that would defeat and destroy us, or are so precious and important to us, we are reminded that only He is strong enough to carry us through each day, and He is the source of all that is good in our lives. We cast our burdens upon Him in the confident belief that He will bear them for us. And we acknowledge Him as the giver of every good and perfect gift. As we do, we not only tap into the rich wellspring of His everlasting love, and practice the sweet discipline of adoring the Lord, but we steer away from the icebergs of self-reliance that can so easily rip open the hull of our coracle of faith. The more we come to God, the less will be our propensity to depend upon our own wisdom, wiles, or will when push comes to shove in the hard places of life. Because prayer keeps us mindful of our need to depend on the Lord and not ourselves, we ought to give more time to prayer.

PRAYER LETS US BE OURSELVES – SAFELY

Prayer is the only place I know where I can be completely myself – in all my wretchedness, filthiness, foolishness, and ignorance – and not be judged for it. There is no condemnation for those who are in Christ Jesus;[15] so, when we come to our heavenly Father in His name, He certainly is not going to condemn us, no matter how feeble or faltering our approach to Him.

In prayer we are free to bring forth the dirty laundry of our most secret sins.[16] We can be as angry or as hilariously happy as we like.[17] We can talk to God about people who have injured us, and ask Him to redress the wrong.[18] We can expose our wildest dreams and greatest hopes to the Lord, whereas our friends or family might consider us ambitious, foolish, or out of our minds.[19] In prayer we can sing, weep, shout, clap our hands, dance a jig, or throw ourselves face down on the ground before the Lord! And, frankly, we all need a little of that at times. Where else can you do such things and not have someone either restrain, rebuke, or report you? We ought to pray more than we do, for prayer is the only safe context in which we can be completely ourselves before a God Who loves and accepts us on the basis of His grace, and not our worthiness. And only as we are truly ourselves before Him will we be able to experience His power to shape our lives more in the direction of His pleasure. Knowing that God has provided a program for prayer that both accommodates our honesty and works to transform us into the image of Christ, we should eagerly apply ourselves to this discipline with greater frequency and fervor.

PRAYER SATISFIES OUR NEED FOR FELLOWSHIP

The psalmist expresses the deep-seated need of every human soul when he writes, "As a deer pants for flowing streams, so pants my soul for you, O God."[20] Augustine captured this deep longing in his familiar prayer, "Thou hast created us for thyself, and our heart cannot be quieted till it may find repose in thee."[21] We are made for God, not merely to know Him, but to enjoy rich and prolonged fellowship with Him. To enter into the beauty of His presence and to experience His glory. To find in Him the deeply satisfying relationship our souls long for, and to grow in that relationship more and more each day. Something deep within us is incomplete apart from this fellowship with our Maker and Redeemer.

There are many ways to enjoy that fellowship, but they all tie into prayer. We rejoice in the presence of God in worship as well as in our times of studying His Word. But that fellowship is never complete if it is merely one way, God reaching down to us. Only as we respond in prayer to Him do we find the satisfaction of knowing that He cares enough to listen to us and to address our needs and concerns. As we hear ourselves speaking to Him as our Father, and as we celebrate His goodness and lovingkindness, His majesty and power, we bask in the sweet delight of His fellowship and know more deeply the great privilege and blessing it is to come into His very presence without fear. We can never find complete rest and peace apart from consistent fellowship with God, and we will never find that fellowship more richly than in prayer. Knowing that God, in the abundance of His grace, has. Master-crafted a program of prayer designed to help us realize that fellowship to the fullest extent, we must eagerly submit to that program, and follow it assiduously, if we would know His blessings.

PRAYER IS THE WAY TO KNOW GREAT AND HIDDEN THINGS

"Call to me and I will answer you, and will tell you great and hidden things that you have not known."[22] Thus God invites us to seek from Him the satisfaction of our every need. He knows exactly what we need, even before we come to Him;[23] yet, He is not likely to satisfy those needs apart from prayer.[24] Too many Christians live unsatisfying, unfulfilled lives – grumpy, gloomy, and disappointed because they feel God has not enriched them as He should, or, at least, as they might like. Yet if we examine the prayers of these believers we will likely find either that their prayers are sorely lacking, framed in such a way as merely to satisfy their every lust and whim,[25] or saturated with doubt and unbelief.[26] When we have learned to pray as God intends, following the program He has prescribed in His Word, and with the motives and intents that are pleasing to Him, He will open up to us blessings so rich and abundant that we will hardly be able to contain them.[27]

PRAYER MAINTAINS THE DEVIL'S DEFEAT

The Lord Jesus Christ has thoroughly defeated the devil and his fiendish allies.[28] His perfect righteousness and saving death avail for our shortcomings, and His resurrection from the dead is the proof that God receives Him as our Justifier. Even now Jesus intercedes for us at the Father's right hand, making our needs and requests known through His blood and righteousness.[29] When we turn to prayer we hold the ground the Lord has gained in His victory over the devil. Prayer is a powerful weapon in the armamentarium of the Lord.[30] It keeps us in touch with our Commander-in-Chief; focuses our attention on His glorious throne and victory; drowns out the distracting voice of our adversary; and sends him on his way looking for someone else to devour.[31]

The believer who does not practice prayer, or whose practice of prayer is intermittent and unsatisfying, has none of these advantages. He will be often tempted and easily drawn into sin, thus giving the spiritual forces of wickedness in high places temporary reason to rejoice before their final, crushing defeat at the return of the Lord.

Through prayer we frustrate the devil's attempts to claim some victory in the midst of his calamitous defeat. Prayer enables us to maintain his humiliation as well as to further our own progress in the life of faith.

PRAYER STRENGTHENS FAITH AND ASSURANCE

There are six reasons why this is so. Consider all that is involved in the very act of prayer: First, in prayer we demonstrate that we believe there is a God Who hears such prayers. Second, we testify that we believe He actually listens to us. Third, we bear witness to the reality of communion with the God of heaven and earth, that is, that we are able to come into His presence without fear of annihilation because of His grace and forgiveness. Fourth, we demonstrate belief in God's concern for our mundane affairs, that He cares enough to take an active interest in our daily needs. Fifth, by coming in Jesus' name, that is, through His blood and righteousness, we recall His perfect work on our behalf, by which alone we have attained salvation with the Lord. Sixth, and related to this, prayer reminds us that nothing we do can make us acceptable to God, that we are totally dependent upon His mercy and grace, and, therefore, He is always willing to receive us because of His lovingkindness and not because of our worthiness. Any discipline which can regularly remind us of these things ought certainly to have a priority in our time.

Being reminded of such things, as we are whenever we pray, we cannot help but grow stronger in our assurance of salvation and in faith. The more we pray the more we are reminded of these great truths, and the more we demonstrate our belief in them and in the God Who works through such means to bless and grow us. The more help we can receive in increasing our prayers and in making them more effective, the more perfectly and completely we will be convinced of these truths and will bask in the assurance of salvation and the joyous life of faith they provide. That God Himself has provided us a program for praying in such a way as continuously to strengthen our faith and increase our assurance ought to give us great joy.

PRAYER HELPS US GET BEYOND THE FLESH

Most of us do not live lives of high adventure and romance. If anything, we regard our lives as fairly routine. We crawl out of bed in the morning, get ourselves ready for the day, head off to work or school, drag ourselves through our daily routines, come home, eat, read the papers or watch TV, and just barely make it to bed before we crash, exhausted. Life, in short, can be rather dull and mundane at times – indeed, perhaps much of the time.

Given this situation, we tend to harbor rather low expectations about what our lives might be like. Most of us do not envision ourselves as great saints of the Lord, leading the charge for His army against the forces of darkness in the advancement of His Kingdom. We consider ourselves to be rather ordinary followers of the Lord who are merely trying to hold down our place in the Lord's tent, doing whatever comes our way as well as we can, given the limitations of our flesh. We do not eagerly anticipate coming face-to-face with the glory of God, knowing the power of God working in us to transform us into the image of Jesus Christ, or seeing our attitudes, hopes, and practices change dramatically over time. We consider ourselves just ordinary people living ordinary lives.

Too bad.

We serve a God Who is able to do exceeding abundantly above all that we could ever think or ask.[32] The problem for most Christians is that they hardly ever think of themselves as servants of such a God with unlimited potential to be used for His glory. They have not learned how to tap into the power that is at work within them for a fuller and more abundant life in Christ. And, since they hardly ever think such lofty thoughts, they don't bother to ask God to make them true for them. Most of us would never think of praying, like John Knox, "Lord, give me Scotland (or my neighborhood, workplace, or school), or I die!" We can't imagine ourselves as anything other than what we have always known ourselves to be – unexceptional people living routine lives and just barely making it at that. How different from this is the Lord's view of us:

> But you are a chosen race, a royal priesthood, a holy nation, a people for his own possession, that you may proclaim the excellencies of him who called you out of darkness into his marvelous light. Once you were not a people, but now you are God's people; once you had not received mercy, but now you have received mercy.[33]

Prayer provides a context in which we can escape the limitations of our flesh. In prayer our vision of God is enlarged, especially when we pray in words that He Himself provides us, as He guides us to think of Him and speak with Him as we ought. As our vision of God expands, our experience of His glorious presence deepens, and our sense of what He is capable of doing in, through, and with us grows as well. We become bolder, more confident in our approach to Him, more willing to ask great things of Him, and more likely to believe that He will answer them. As we begin to pray this way we become more alert to opportunities for serving the Lord throughout the day, and more willing to step into the gap as His servants and witnesses. Our faith grows; we know more of the power and joy of the Lord; life becomes an adventure even in the midst of mundane circumstances; and our prayers continue to grow bolder and more confident.

Prayer, when entered into according to the program the Lord has provided, using words that He Himself has given us, can help us to get beyond the limitations of our flesh to know more of the full and abundant life for which we have been saved by our Lord Jesus Christ.

PRAYER FULFILLS GOD'S PURPOSE FOR CREATION

Genesis 1 is clear that God intended the creation for His own glory and delight. He made what He did, as He did, to bring pleasure to Himself. This is the meaning of the many times in Genesis 1 that God looked upon all that He had made and described it as "good." He was pleased with it, and He is pleased when He sees that goodness continuing in His creation.

That God is pleased when we pray should be obvious, if only from the fact that He has commanded us to pray, as we noted above. As we pray we are pleasing God, doing something He regards as good, and, thus, fulfilling at least part of His purpose for us, His creatures, and for His creation as a whole. As we intercede for others we seek the Lord's good for them, thus helping to realize His purpose for their lives as well. And as the power that flows to us from prayer begins to be expressed in all our roles, relationships, and responsibilities, the goodness of God begins to be realized more and more in every area of our lives, thus bringing glory to God and pleasing Him.

Prayer helps us in bringing the purposes of creation to fulfillment before the Lord, such that His goodness abounds more and more in our lives and throughout His creation as a result of our prayers. It may be difficult to see how this is so, but the teaching of Scripture throughout is that God is both pleased when His people pray and pleased to act according to His good pleasure in response to their prayers. Prayer helps to fulfill God's good plan for His creation.

PRAYER IS TRANSFORMATIONAL

Consider just a few of the things that Scripture tells us are possible as a result of prayer:[34] Our daily needs will be met through prayer. We can know peace in the midst of trouble.[35] We can move beyond guilt and shame to become powerful witnesses for the Lord.[36] The eyes of our hearts can be opened so that we can understand more of God's Word and experience more of His power.[37] We can live in a manner worthy of the Lord, be pleasing to Him in all respects, and bear much fruit for His glory.[38] Who among the followers of Jesus does not desire such a life? Yet it is not likely that any of these great blessings will be ours apart from prayer. But through prayer – ours and the prayers of those who intercede for us – we can surely know more of the transforming power of God at work in our lives. No prayer, no growth; much prayer, and prayer in the context of

God's own designed and prescribed program of prayer, and nothing is impossible for us.[39]

Prayer is a critical component in Christian growth, so we ought to learn as much as we can about how to pray as we should.

PRAYER MAKES US MORE LIKE JESUS

It is the burden of God's Spirit, working in us by means of the Word of God, to transform us increasingly into the very image of Jesus Christ our Lord.[40] In this life we are to become more like Him and less like ourselves, as John the Baptist observed: "He must increase, but I must decrease."[41] That Jesus was often given to prayer is clear from the testimonies of the evangelists. The more we pray, the more we reflect the work of God's Spirit, transforming us into the very image of Jesus. If we want to be like Jesus in our public lives – caring for others, serving them, bearing witness to the Kingdom of God – we shall have to work harder to become like Him in our private lives.

Prayer was a powerful source of daily strength for the Lord, as we have seen. As we grow in prayer, and as our prayers become a more powerful and meaningful part of our lives, we will begin to be more like Jesus, both in our prayers, and in our daily walk. So intent is our heavenly Father on seeing this happen in us that He has provided a marvelous and powerfully effective program of prayer to help this transformation come to pass.

PRAYER IS THE WAY TO KNOW PEACE

How do we respond to trials? Wring our hands? Fret and worry? Complain to others? Get angry? Get even? Shrivel up and lay low? However we respond, all these are efforts to try to restore peace to our troubled lives. When trials beset us we want nothing more than to recover the equilibrium – the peace – that obtained in our lives before the trouble came upon us. So whether we worry or get angry or just sit and sulk, we're doing what we think will make us feel better, what will restore our peace.

Scripture tells us that prayer is the surest way to know such peace.[42] But not just any kind of prayer. It must be prayer coupled with thanksgiving, with praising and thanking the Lord *in the midst* of the trial, *for* the trial, *and in the confident belief that even this is being worked together for His good in our lives.*[43] We may not feel like giving thanks, but we are not commanded to feel thankful, only to give thanks. We can give thanks to God as an act of faith, believing that He is sovereign in all the affairs of our lives, that He loves and cares for us, and that He will bring good out of this difficulty, even if it takes a long time. Thus we may need to practice thanksgiving for an extended period of time, indeed, continuously. I recall once hearing a woman's sad story of unremitting depression, and how she had tried every remedy and consulted numerous physicians for some relief. At the end of her long account, I asked, "Have you thanked God for your depression?" She became immediately indignant and said, "That's abnormal!" Precisely. It is normal for us to worry about everything, pray about nothing, and complain without ceasing. But God counsels us to follow a different tack. As we pray with thanksgiving, focusing on the trials that come our way, Paul promises that the peace of God will come over us in ways we can't even understand, and we will be able to bear up under our trial in the grace of the Lord. Prayer is the surest way to know peace in the midst of trials.

PRAYER KEEPS US IN FOCUS

How easy it is to become distracted by all the mundane activity that characterizes our lives. Every day, as we slog through our routines, we are confronted by the materialism, hedonism, sensuality, and temporality of the world in which we live. We could easily come to believe that this life is what matters most, and that we should devote the better part of our energies to getting the most out of this life while we can. But Paul counsels us otherwise. He tells us to set our hearts and minds on the things of the Lord, to keep the vision of Christ exalted and enthroned before our eyes throughout the day, and to do all that we do in such a way as to represent Him as ambassadors of His Kingdom.[44] This is the full and abundant life to which we have been called.

Prayer can be a great help to us in this calling, especially if, following the Lord's program, we establish different times throughout the day to come before His throne of grace. Prayer is like a compass for our spirits when so used, allowing us to check our course, set our sails, and keep our bearings as the seas of secularity threaten to wash over the decks of our lives. Prayer keeps us focused on who we really are, rather than who we might seem to be in the midst of a materialistic age. Prayer allows us, as was said of St Brigid, to "practice the life of heaven on earth" and know the power of eternity breaking into our present experience, more and more each day.

PRAYER SETS US APART

It always thrills and pleases me when, in a restaurant, I see other people around me praying over their meals. I feel a kinship with those praying folks, even though I don't know them by name or anything else about them. I have often taken the time, as I was leaving the restaurant, to commend them for their prayers, and have always been warmly received in return. People who pray in public announce to the world that they're different. We are set apart together from the rest of humanity by the fact that we acknowledge our dependence upon the Lord. The same is true of those who pray in private. And for those who make more time in their daily lives for prayer in the midst of all their other occupations.

In a day when it seems that very little, apart from some differences in our weekly routine, distinguishes the followers of Christ from the rest of the world, prayer does – or can. The fact that we pray makes us different. We recognize an authority, a source, and a hope beyond ourselves, beyond this life and world, to which we submit and on which we depend for our daily sustenance, guidance, and strength. The Bible calls those who are followers of Christ, "saints." The word means literally, "set apart ones." We have been set apart unto God and for His purposes in the world. Prayer is an important way that we maintain and express our "set-apartness."

God desires to make the most of this "set-apartness," and has designed a program of prayer that will help to make us stand out as lights in the world. Ask yourself this: Does the fact that Muslims pray at set times of the day, stopping what they are doing to kneel and bow in a certain direction – does this set them apart, make them stand out from the rest of the world? What if God has something like this in mind for us?

PRAYER PREPARES US FOR THE LORD'S RETURN

The Apostle Peter wrote, "The end of all things is at hand; therefore, be self-controlled and sober-minded for the sake of your prayers."[45] It is true: "The End Is Near!" Everything that we are familiar with is about to be consumed by the fiery wrath of God and done away with in preparation for the new heavens and the new earth. All the great heroes, the large corporations, the huge military arsenals and national governments, even all the things that cause us fear and concern. They are all, every day, drawing nearer to their end.

How should we prepare for this cosmic calamity? Peter tells us by getting our heads on straight and notching our spirits into a mode of prayer. As the return of our Lord approaches, nearer every day, we need to be praying more, and praying more effectively, if we are going to be ready for His sudden return. But how can we do that if we don't know how to pray as we should? God's prayer program can help us to fulfill Peter's charge and prepare ourselves more effectively for the glorious return of the Savior.

PRAYER ENGAGES US WITH GOD

There is nothing quite like prayer to bring us fully into the presence of God, to enable us to know His presence and help in all its rich fullness. In prayer we enter the very throne-room of the Father, by His invitation, for the purpose of bringing our requests to Him and finding grace to help in our times of need.[46] As we enter, the Son of God, our great High Priest, rises at the Father's right hand, to welcome us and to advocate our needs to His Father and ours.[47] And when we begin to speak, not knowing how to pray as we ought, the Spirit of God Himself intercedes for us, using language appropriate to the setting, and bearing our requests before the Lord in power.[48] In no other aspect of the life of faith are we as fully engaged with the Persons of the Godhead as in prayer. What a rich privilege and great blessing for those who resort to it often!

Once we understand these seventeen reasons why we should pray there will never again be any doubt but that mastering the discipline of prayer is something to which every Christian must devote himself. The excuses that keep us from prayer will pale into nothingness as we draw on these many reasons to pray and take up the program God has prepared for us.

But knowing these reasons for prayer does not make mastering prayer any easier. For that, we need more help still.

QUESTIONS FOR STUDY OR DISCUSSION

1. Which of the excuses for not praying have you heard yourself give? Do you find those excuses – and not praying – truly satisfying? Why or why not?

2. Review the seventeen reasons for praying. Which of those have you found to be true? Explain.

3. Which of those seventeen reasons for praying have you yet to experience? Would you like to?

4. Given what prayer is capable of in our lives – those seventeen reasons to pray – how would you assess your practice of prayer at this time? On a scale of 1 to 10, 10 being "Completely Satisfying," what number would you assign your prayer life? Why?

5. Set some goals for this study of God's prayer program. What do you hope to learn? How do you want your practice of prayer to improve? What will tell you, at the end of this study, that this was a worthwhile experience?

---

[1] Abraham Kuyper, *Lectures on Calvinism* (Grand Rapids: Eerdmans, 1970), p. 20.
[2] Matthew 4:1-11.

[3] An earlier version of this chapter appeared in my book, *Disciplines of Grace* (Downers Grove, IL: InterVarsity Press, 2001), pp. 76ff.

[4] Genesis 4:26.

[5] Romans 4:9-16.

[6] Genesis 12:7, 8; 13:18.

[7] Genesis 19:27: The Hebrew form of the verb, he stood, used in conjunction with the relative pronoun, suggests a habitual practice on Abraham's part.

[8] cf. Psalms 51, 3, 25.

[9] Galatians 4:6. In fact, from the Greek, it is clear in this passage that it is the Holy Spirit Who does this crying out to God as our Father, thus setting a pattern of His helping us in prayer even from the beginning of our walk with the Lord.

[10] Revelation 8:3, 4.

[11] Psalm 50:14, 15.

[12] Jeremiah 33:3.

[13] Matthew 7:7.

[14] Saint Augustine, *The City of God*, Vol. I, Book III, Ch. XIV. Tr. by John Healey, ed. by R. V. G. Tasker (London: Everyman's Library, 1967), p. 89.

[15] Romans 8:1.

[16] Psalm 90:8.

[17] cf. Psalms 137, 150.

[18] Psalm 109.

[19] Psalm 89.

[20] Psalm 42:1.

[21] St Augustine, *Confessions*, William Watts, tr. (Cambridge: Harvard University Press, 1989), p. 3.

[22] Jeremiah 33:3.

[23] Matthew 6:8.

[24] James 4:2.

[25] James 4:3.

[26] James 1:5-7.

[27] Malachi 3:10; Ephesians 3:20.

[28] Matthew 12:22-29; Colossians 2:8-15.

[29] 1 John 2:1, 2; Heb. 7:25.

[30] Ephesians 6:10-20.

[31] 1 Peter 5:8.

[32] Ephesians 3:20.

[33] 1 Peter 2:9, 10.

[34] Matthew 6:11; 7:8.

[35] Philippians 4:6, 7.

[36] Psalm 51:10-15.

[37] Ephesians 1:15-19.
[38] Colossians 1:9, 10.
[39] cf. Mark 9:14-29.
[40] 2 Corinthians 3:17, 18.
[41] John 3:30
[42] Philippians 4:6, 7
[43] Romans 8:28
[44] Colossians 3:1-3; 1 Corinthians 10:31; 2 Corinthians 5:17-20
[45] 1 Peter 4:7
[46] Hebrews 4:16
[47] Acts 7:55; Hebrews 4:14, 15; 1 John 2:1
[48] Romans 8:26, 27

2.

A Venerable Program

Now what is there to do? It is to have songs not merely honest but also holy, which will be like spurs to incite us to pray to God and to praise Him, and to meditate upon His works in order to love, fear, honor, and glorify Him...Wherefore, although we look far and wide and search on every hand, we shall not find better songs nor songs better suited to that end than the Psalms of David which the Holy Spirit made and uttered through him. And for this reason, when we sing them we may be certain that God puts the words in our mouths as if He Himself sang in us to exalt His glory.

-John Calvin[1]

God has gone up with a shout, the LORD with the sound of a trumpet. Sing praises to God, sing praises! Sing praises to our King, sing praises! For God is the King of all the earth; sing praises with a psalm!

- Psalm 47:5-7

O God, exalted on high, exalted over the nations, Lord Jesus Christ, kings and Lord of lords, I praise and worship you with my voice and with my song! You only are King and Lord; let all the peoples of the earth be brought to praise You, O Lord! Let all who know and love You lift up their voices and praise You with psalms!

Of all the books of Scripture none is more familiar or better loved than the Psalms. The 150 psalms of this great book have been a source of comfort, strength, encouragement, and guidance to believers of every generation, every nation, and every walk of life.

They have been a tool of devotion for monks and laymen alike. Believers from all walks of life have sung and prayed them throughout the day. The Church has used the psalms to celebrate the reviving grace of God. Troops have gone into war with psalms on their lips, praying that God would teach their hands to do battle and shelter them under His wings. The psalms have brought peace and hope in times of trouble, doubt, or loss to saints of all generations. Here all the great themes of Scripture meet in glorious poetry to celebrate the grace of the Lord and His faithfulness to His people. In these songs, prayers, and declarations of faith, some of the richest Messianic prophecies may be found – of Christ's suffering, death, resurrection, and reign, in particular. The psalms plumb the depths of human emotion, and invite us to bring all our affections out into the open before the Lord. The whole work of the Church, and the entirety of the walk of faith are explored in this great prayer book of the Church. In the New Testament the psalms provided a rich source of doctrinal truth, aiding the apostles in assembling the foundational teachings concerning man's sin and God's redeeming grace. The psalms have been and remain today a rich resource of comfort, guidance, and strength for believers of every generation and all walks of life.

But, over the years, the psalms have served primarily in another role, one which has come to be largely overlooked by vast numbers of Christians in our generation. That is as the hymnbook of the people of God, the primary resource for praise and prayer for our times of corporate worship. For more than two thousand years the psalms have constituted a venerable program of prayer and worship for the followers of Jesus Christ. In this chapter I want to introduce the reader to the Book of Psalms. It is quite possible that many may not understand the composition, character, and purpose of these 150 songs, prayers, and declarations of faith. Recently Susie and I were having dinner with a couple who are leaders in a local community Bible study ministry, involving hundreds of men and women. They have taught and led groups in this ministry for many years, and are recognized as faithful teachers. However, when the subject of the psalms came up as we were advising them how to pray about a particular situation, they both confessed that, not only had they never studied the psalter, they had not even read it all the way through, and had no idea it might serve them as a guide for their prayers. So, in the first place, in this chapter I want to give you something of the flavor and purpose of the Book of Psalms. Second, however, I want to provide an overview of the ways the psalms have been used in worship by the people of God in all ages. Very few readers will have much experience in allowing their worship of God to be led by the psalms. I want to show historically why the Church has believed this to be important, then explain some of my own experience in using the psalms in corporate worship. We'll see that what God has provided His Church to guide her corporate worship will only bear its most vital fruit in that context as these songs, prayers, and confessions of faith become the foundation of our own program of prayer as well. We'll look first at the psalms themselves.

THE BOOK OF PSALMS[2]

The largest book in the Bible, Psalms also explores the widest range of themes, involves the broadest collection of authors, and takes us through the widest spectrum of emotions of any of the books of the Bible.

Authorship

Throughout their history the people of Israel delighted to honor and worship God with psalms. The Book of Psalms reflects the record of Israel's history, from redemption to exile. While many of the psalms were written by David, a number of other authors were involved as well. Second to David in number of psalms is Asaph, who served as one of David's worship leaders.[3] His twelve psalms (50, 73-83) reflect a deep concern for purity in Israel, both personally and in the nation as a whole. The sons of Korah, gatekeepers in the Temple[4] who, like Asaph, appear to have been part of a Davidic/Solomonic worship team, also contributed a number of psalms, especially 42-49. Psalms are included that were written by Heman (88) and Ethan (89), other members of David's worship leaders,[5] and by Moses (90). Psalm 105 may have been composed by someone in Joshua's generation, given the historical moment in which it seems to have been written, while Psalm 137 clearly reflects on the experience of Israel's being held captive in Babylon. There are also a large number of psalms to which authorship is not ascribed. Many of these are of the character of the psalms attributed to David, and so are regarded by many as having been written by him as well.

Thus, from the authorship alone we can see that the practice of psalm-writing goes back to the earliest days of Israel's history, the time of Moses, although the period most conducive to psalm-writing appears to have been during the reigns of David and Solomon, when Israel was at the height of her national glory. At this time a unique combination of circumstances – David's musical and poetical skills, the preparation for and building of the temple, and a long season of peace and prosperity among them – combined to encourage the writing of many, if not most, of the songs, prayers, and confessions of faith in the psalter.

Purpose

Psalms were written for various purposes or occasions. For example, Psalm 30 was intended for the dedication of the house, perhaps the temple of the Lord, according to the superscription accompanying it. Psalms 32, 38, and 51 were written to express contrition for sin and rededication to the Lord. Psalm 92 was intended for use on the Sabbath day; Psalm 102 as a cry for the afflicted; Psalms 120-134 for singing on the way up to Jerusalem and the

Temple for worship; and Psalm 145 as a general song of praise. There are psalms to help us when we are down (43), in praying for missionaries (67), to remind us of our call to righteousness (1), and to guide us in understanding God's Word (19, 119).

We should perhaps say a word about the superscriptions that accompany many of the psalms. Scholars are divided on how to regard these, that is, whether they should be considered as inspired and therefore parts of the psalms themselves, or as later editorial insertions. The Hebrew Bible incorporates them into the text of the psalms they accompany. For this reason, the verse numbering of psalms with superscriptions in the Hebrew Bible differs from that of our English Bibles. In addition to providing information on authorship, the superscriptions are intended to tell us about the circumstances of the composition of the psalm (3, 18, 51); to provide directions in how to play or sing them (4, 5, 53), including recommendations for instrumentation, particular neumes (melody lines) to follow, or even popular tunes to which the psalm can be sung; or to tell us about the particular character of the psalm, whether it is for praise, to guide in learning wisdom, or for singing. My own view is that it is best, whenever superscriptions appear, to consider them carefully and to use whatever benefit they provide in helping us to understand the psalm. Especially when we are praying a psalm that has a superscription it can be helpful in establishing a mood, context, or focus for our prayer to spend a few moments reflecting on the information conveyed in the superscription, that we might better understand the purpose of the psalm.

Emotional range

The various psalms lead us to experience a wide range of emotions: warning (1, 2), pleading (5), urgency (7), trouble (13), remorse (51), rejection (60), despair (88), exultation (99), and many more. Some psalms even lead us through great changes in mood during the course of the psalm itself. For example, Psalm 43 begins with a feeling of rejection and being mistreated, only to turn to self-rebuke, hope, and praise before it is finished. Psalm 13 begins in a feeling of hopelessness and near panic and resolves into one of confidence and praise. This exploration of the affective side of human nature makes Psalms a very human book, allowing us to be ourselves before the Lord without fearing that He will judge or condemn us. The Psalms start where we are and teach us how to find refuge in the Lord, regardless of our emotional state, so that we may rest and rejoice in Him. They also help us to accept and appreciate the role of affections in helping us grow in our relationship with the Lord.

Subjects

The Psalms also presents us with a wide range of subjects. Indeed, almost anything we can think to pray about is broached in these songs, hymns, prayers, and confessions of faith in the Lord, including, missions (67), church growth (147), the beauty and wonder of the creation (19, 104), human purpose (8), the role of governors and other rulers (72, 82), the need for revival (80), the wellbeing of communities and families (127), and all manner of individual needs. They also give us the most complete picture of God Himself, showing Him to us as Creator (100, 104), sovereign Ruler of all He has made (93), Redeemer of His people (95, 105), Judge of all men (50, 96), glorious, splendid, powerful, and wise in all He is and does (50, 111). In particular, the Psalms anticipate the work of Christ Himself for the salvation of God's people, pointing to His suffering (22), His vicarious atonement (69), His resurrection (16), and the celebration of His eternal reign (2). Messianic themes and foretastes appear in many of the psalms. At the same time, we may say that all the psalms are Messianic, in that they ultimately lead to Christ Himself – as, indeed, do all the Scriptures.[6]

Form

The Psalms, of course, are written in the form of poetry, but not, perhaps, as most of us are inclined to think about that particular genre. That is, we do not find much in the way of rhyming of sounds or consistent metrical structuring in the psalms. We can recognize individual verses and even, in some cases, stanzas. But, for the most part, this is only because our English Bible editors have set the text up to facilitate our reading. The Hebrew Bible offers little such help.

Yet the psalms are poetry in that we find in them the use of familiar poetic devices, such as, hyperbole, allusion, metaphor, and others. Considerable attention is also given in the psalms to the rhyming of thoughts, using various kinds of parallelism, one line restating, opposing, or enlarging upon the line before it in order to dramatize, emphasize, or clarify a point or idea. Wherever parallelism occurs the various thoughts included must be taken together as expressing one idea. The effect is thus to make that idea stronger and more compelling.

Some psalms (such as 112, 113, and 119) are acrostics. Each line, or verse, or stanza of the psalm begins with the next letter in sequence of the Hebrew alphabet. This device was used to enhance the beauty and memorability of the psalm in a culture in which literacy and written texts were not widespread.

Types

The Psalms are also of various types. In particular, we can identify wisdom psalms, or, psalms in which the way of the wise man is compared or contrasted with that of the fool (1, 14). These are intended to instruct us in how to live in a manner pleasing to the Lord. Kingly psalms celebrate, describe, or invoke the rule of God's king or God Himself over His people and the nations (2, 47, 110). These psalms help us both in understanding the role of rulers before the Lord and the nature of God's Kingdom. In psalms of complaint (13, 52) the speaker is seeking God's help against some foe or in the midst of some trial. Psalms of praise and thanksgiving are intended to guide and facilitate our practice of these disciplines (149, 150).

Testimony psalms are declarations of trust in God, often in the form of rehearsals of His mighty acts (104, 105). They remind us of God's faithfulness to His people, His sovereign care of His creation, or His rule over the nations. Psalms of confession (38, 32, 51) help us in keeping a clean slate before the Lord, and psalms of admonition warn of judgment from God for behavior that is not pleasing to Him (50). We can see how even the various types of psalms can be useful to us in worship and prayer.

Arrangement

The 150 psalms in the psalter are arranged in five books, Psalms 1-41, 42-72, 73-89, 90-106 and 107-150. Scholars are not certain just how these various divisions arose, but that they are present is clear. This dividing of the psalter may have been accomplished some time after the exile to Babylon and return to Jerusalem during the later period of Old Testament history. The division seems to reflect a sort of progress in the psalms. The first of the five books, for example, contains many psalms of complaint (as well as many other kinds), while the last book consists mainly of psalms of testimony and praise. Many of the early psalms are individual psalms, while most of the later ones are corporate. The mood of the early books is frequently one of distress and pleading (although not exclusively, of course), while the later psalms are mostly of praise. Whoever arranged the psalms may have intended to represent the journey of faith from initial trust and understanding, to the beginnings of growth and development, through the maturity of continuous thanks and praise. While this is not certain, the contents of the five books and the pattern of their overall arrangement suggest some such thinking.

The Psalms are a rich treasury from which to draw for our worship and our lives. As we become more familiar with the various psalms and begin to use them in our prayers, we will find they actually begin to become part of our lives, allowing us to accept ourselves as we are, but challenging us to grow in grace and in love for the Lord Who has given us this wonderful compilation of songs, prayers, hymns, and confessions to use in approaching His throne of grace.

USE OF THE PSALMS IN PRAYER AND WORSHIP

Beginning in the Scriptures themselves, and continuing on into the history of the Church, we can find numerous examples of the faithful using the psalms in worship. For the most part, those psalms seem to arise spontaneously, in the midst of other prayers or as the framework within which prayers are offered. This suggests that those psalms were so well known – perhaps through disciplined daily use – that they could easily be drawn on to inform the prayers of God's people when their own words simply did not seem to do the job – when they did not know how to pray as they ought.

Praying psalms in the Old Testament

David, for example, at the end of his life, offered a lengthy prayer in praise to God for all His mercy and grace. That prayer draws liberally from many of the psalms, not all of them clearly his own.[7] Solomon incorporated psalms freely into his majestic prayer of dedication for the Temple.[8] Hezekiah and Daniel did the same at critical periods in their own ministries.[9] Hezekiah, at the beginning of a period of national revival, instructed the Levites to use the psalms in leading the people into renewed worship of God.[10] In Daniel 9:5 the prophet used the words of Psalm 106:6 to declare his and his people's guilt before the Lord and to seek His renewing grace. Jonah also used the psalms for his prayers at a crucial moment. In Jonah 2 the prophet records his near-death experience, in which he cries out to the Lord in his distress and seeks to recover his mission. In his desperation, it was the psalms that came to his lips.[11] All these Old Testament saints must have had a ready familiarity with the psalms, perhaps developed through the discipline of regular praying through the psalter, in order to be able so freely to draw from the psalms during these special times of prayer.

Praying psalms in the New Testament

The same appears to be the case in the New Testament. In Acts 1, when the 120 disciples were assembled together in that upper room for united prayer, Peter suddenly interrupted their prayers to lead the people in selecting a replacement for Judas. I believe this was because, as they were praying through the psalter, they came upon Ps. 69:25, which reminded Peter of Ps. 109:8 (to which they had perhaps not yet come) in which are found the words that Peter quotes in Acts 1:20, and which led to a temporary interruption in the prayer meeting. This practice of looking to the psalms and invoking or involving them in prayer can also be clearly seen in the account in Acts 4 of the believers facing up to the first threat of persecution. When the apostles returned from their hearing before the Jewish leaders and reported their threats and warning, the whole congregation of God's people, with one voice, turned to God in prayer. Using first Psalm 146:6 to address the Lord, they then prayed from Psalm 2:1, 2 in order to introduce their supplication before Him. How were they able so readily to use these exact words? All of them together, with one voice? It could only have been through a long-standing familiarity with these prayers, developed as part of a program of personal spiritual discipline during their nurture in the Jewish community. In Acts 16 we read that Paul and Silas, in the Philippian jail, were "praying a hymn", as the Greek has it in v. 25. Following the earthquake the jailer rushed up and asked, "What must I do to be saved?" Why did he ask Paul and Silas about salvation? Probably because they were singing about salvation, praying perhaps Psalm 67, which is titled as a hymn in the superscription, and of the ten psalms that are thus titled, seems most to celebrate the saving power of God. In Ephesians 5:18, 19 the Apostle Paul tells us that one of the marks of Spirit-filled people is that they sing among (or to – the Greek is flexible) themselves in psalms. So familiar are Spirit-filled people with the Book of Psalms, and so much do they delight in and benefit from them, that in and among themselves they resort to singing the psalms (along with other hymns and spiritual songs) as a source of refreshment and strengthening for their souls.

The Biblical precedent seems abundantly clear: God's people used the psalms in their prayers. They were able and wont to do so in their times of worship together no doubt because, individually, they had submitted to a disciplined approach to learning and using the psalms in their daily prayers. The Book of Psalms served a vital foundational role in their program of personal spiritual discipline.

Praying the psalms throughout Church history
This pattern continues into the early centuries of Church history.[12] It was the singing of psalms by the Christians in Milan that began to penetrate the hard heart of the worldly Augustine.[13] Later on, he recommended the regular praying of psalms for those who were under his care in the city of Hippo.[14] The desert fathers of the third and fourth centuries established a precedent of regularly praying through the psalms that was taken up by monks and pastors throughout the Middle Ages.[15] In the Celtic tradition boys who were set apart for the priesthood from an early age learned to pray the psalms as a first stage of their training. Brendan, for example, could pray the entire psalter by memory by the time he was ten.[16] Columba had learned at least some of the

psalms even before he could read.[17] The liturgical chants which have given order and majesty to the worship of the Church from its earliest years were largely composed of psalms. So also were the "books of hours" – lay devotional guides – developed during the medieval period. The Protestant reformers were not strangers to using the psalms in worship. Luther, Bach, and Schutz put the psalms into the vernacular and adapted them to more familiar and accessible tunes, so that congregations could join together in worshipping the Lord with the psalms. Calvin learned the practice of using the psalms in worship during his stay in Strasbourg, and wrote,

> Furthermore, it is a thing most expedient for the edification of the church to sing some psalms in the form of public prayers by which one prays to God or sings His praises so that the hearts of all may be aroused and stimulated to make similar prayers and to render similar praises and thanks to God with a common love.[18]

The first book published on American soil was the Massachusetts Bay Psalter, building on traditions with which the people were already well acquainted in order to sustain and guide their worship in the new world.

Only in our day does it seem that evangelical Christians have grown unaccustomed to using the psalms in worship. We have departed from Biblical and historical precedent, and set aside God's venerable program, in our preference for simplistic prayer formulas and detailed lists, catchy contemporary choruses, and old familiar hymns. Not that these do not have a place in our personal and corporate worship; it's just that we should not be so quick to substitute these – lock, stock, and barrel – for the prayer list, prayer book, and prayer and worship program that God Himself has provided in the psalms. While we may need these oars of human invention at times to help us navigate the waters of life, we must never furl the sail of the psalms in our prayers, lest we fail to catch the wind of God's Spirit as He carries us along before the throne of grace. If the singing of psalms is an indication that our sails are filled with the wind of the Spirit, then let us undertake to recover this divinely-appointed program of prayer and worship.

But why use the psalms in prayer and worship?
But are there reasons as compelling as Biblical and historical precedent that can encourage us to begin praying the psalms more consistently and more frequently? Why did our forebears in the faith find praying the psalms to be so important to their own life of faith? I can think of at least eight reasons.

(1) First, we know they are pleasing to God. He gave them, and He has preserved them though the ages. God wants His people to worship Him in the ways that He has provided, as the tragedy of Nadab and Abihu reminds us.[19] Having given His people detailed guidelines for how to approach Him in worship, God was not pleased when Aaron's sons took it upon themselves to forsake His guidance and offer something of their own. This same jealousy

for His prescribed ways of worship lies back of God's condemnation of all pagan worship and His prohibition against including any aspects of paganism in the worship offered to Him. We can conclude from this that God, having given us the psalter, would be pleased to hear it used more faithfully by His people in the worship they bring to Him.

(2) Second, the psalms allow us to pray comprehensively. They leave out nothing for which we might come before the Lord in prayer. Every mood and emotion is expressed. All our personal, spiritual, and vocational needs are touched upon. Missions, the work of kings and governors, the growth and development of the Church, the blessings of home, congregation, and nation – all these and more come to light in the psalms as guidelines for our prayers. When we pray the psalms, using the whole of God's prayer program on a regular basis, we can be sure that our prayers will be as comprehensive as possible.

(3) Third, the psalms enable us to pray honestly. They let us look at our sins; they respect our emotional state; they lead us to bring our struggles freely before the Lord; and they allow us to examine the state of our salvation at any given time. It is as though God is coaxing out from us attitudes, sentiments, and admissions that we might otherwise be too fearful or dull to present to Him. Yet in the words of the prayers He has provided for us He helps us to be ourselves before Him, without fear.

(4) Fourth, the psalms help us in praying reflectively, in thinking about our lives from God's perspective,

not merely our own, or a perspective conditioned only by pressing needs. We can reflect on the work of Christ, our individual callings, the kind of character we should be striving to develop, our deepest needs and fears, God's faithfulness to His covenant, our eternal hope, the mission of the Church, and much more, seeing all these from the way God intends them to be seen, and not merely from our fallen, finite point of view. The psalms allow God's vision for our lives to have more priority of place in our minds and hearts as we take His words to guide us in our prayers.

(5) Fifth, the psalms challenge us to pray beyond the limits of our own resources. We do not know how to pray as we ought. The psalms give us the words we need, focus on the subjects with which we should be concerned, and express our prayers with such a majesty and loftiness that they cannot help but stretch and grow us, taking us to ever higher levels of spiritual experience and maturity. The psalms teach us words and phrases to use in praising the Lord that remain with us to guide as we go out from prayer into our daily lives. They guide us in how to believe God, in what we are willing to trust Him for. The psalms stretch us beyond where we are and take us more powerfully to where God wants us to be.

(6) Sixth, and related to the previous reason, the psalms are a faithful stimulus to our imaginations, enlarging our vision and understanding of God and of our calling as His children. It is all too easy when we come before the throne of grace for our

prayers to be limited or circumscribed by the needs of others, our own needs, and our present state of understanding of the Lord. The psalms keep before us a fresh and growing vision of the God we serve and the life to which He has called us as His people, enabling us truly to grow in grace and in the knowledge of Him.

(7) Seventh, praying the psalms regularly reminds us to pray for things we might otherwise neglect, such as, our rulers, the persecuted church, our enemies, the spiritual warfare and all its trials and temptations, the lonely and downcast, the poor and needy, and a host of others. Our own prayer lists might overlook one or more of these, but God's does not. Using His can help us to be more faithful in praying about important matters that we might forget if all we have before us are the lists of our own devising.

(8) Finally, praying the psalms satisfies like nothing else I have ever known. And this must have been true for all those countless saints in previous ages who faithfully prayed through the psalms, so much so that they had them readily available for their spontaneous prayers at critical moments in their lives. This is what we all desire for our prayers, and what we should be striving for as well.

Not long ago I was in a meeting of the local credentialing committee of our denomination, the committee which is charged with examining candidates for the Gospel ministry. During that meeting a candidate shared frankly and openly about his struggles in the faith. He had been through many difficult times, and they were weighing on him still. He was deeply affected, and so was his family. There was much hurt, and there had been much seeking of the Lord's will. The committee went to prayer together for this man. I was stunned by his story and hardly knew what to pray. That must have been true for everyone else as well, because it was a long time before someone finally broke the silence. The first prayer offered came spontaneously from Psalm 30, as a member of the commission prayed in David's words about the weeping that lasts for a night, to be followed by the shout of joy that comes in the morning. I was deeply moved and wondrously satisfied with that prayer. In fact, it was almost the only prayer offered, and seemed to say everything any of the rest of us might have wanted to pray. When we looked up from prayer, the candidate was in tears, but they were tears of hope and joy, as the smile behind them made abundantly clear. This is but a token of the kind of power that can come from learning to adopt God's prayer program as our own.

THE PSALMS IN CORPORATE WORSHIP

I believe that God has given His people the Book of Psalms so that they would use it to approach Him in worship. These words and songs are the ones He is pleased to hear, and the ones we most need, whenever we are before Him. That does not mean that psalms and only psalms must guide us in worship; however, I believe God is pleased when we take up a program – individually and corporately – that makes more use of this resource for worship and prayer.

Imagine that you and I have been appointed as ambassadors to a foreign country. We are preparing to arrive and to have our first audience with the king and his court. We have been given a manual by our government advising us of the protocols, procedures, code of dress, order of proceedings, proper subjects for discussion, and so forth that our new nation has observed for countless generations whenever people assemble in the presence of the king. Now suppose that, for whatever reason – the ways seem too archaic and outmoded, we find the dress code disagreeable, we're not all that interested in what the king wants to discuss, or we simply prefer our own way of speaking and our own order of doing things to what the manual prescribes – we decide to set aside the manual and just do whatever we think is best for us. How successful do you think we will be as ambassadors in this country, and with this king?

It is no different in our worship of the living God. Given the Biblical and historical precedent – the clear testimony of the practice of saints from the Old and New Testaments and the long history of the Church – of using the psalms as the primary program of prayer and worship, how have we in our generation decided simply to set that venerable program aside and do whatever we think is best in approaching the God of heaven and earth? And why, given that we do this so consistently, do we wonder that our own practice of the Christian faith seems to lack the abundance of blessing and power that Scripture holds out to the faithful? Or that the Church in our day continues to become more marginal to the great moral, social, and cultural issues?

In our church we try to make wide use of the psalms in worship. They serve as calls to worship, corporate prayers of confession, and responsive readings. We sing them in old, familiar hymns and newer, livelier praise songs, as well as in versifications of whole psalms set to well-known hymn tunes. We also encourage the people of God to learn how to pray the psalms on their own. Guidebooks for praying the psalms are at the kneeling stations in our prayer room. Various ministries in the church incorporate specific psalms to be prayed as part of their training. Courses have been devoted to teaching people to pray the psalms. The entire Wednesday evening service of worship and prayer is guided and scripted entirely of psalms, and psalms are sung (a capella) and prayed by the congregation as a whole. The people in our congregation, young and old, welcome the psalms and are learning to delight in them and benefit from them. We have encountered no opposition or hesitancy in beginning to use God's prayer program more consistently and broadly in the worship and spiritual disciplines of our church. But then, given that this is God's prayer program, and that the Church in all ages has found it to be advantageous in many ways, why would we?

But how can we learn to pray the psalms, and to use God's program of prayer, so that this rich resource for worship and spiritual growth will be available for us whenever we need it for our prayers?

QUESTIONS FOR STUDY OR DISCUSSION

1. How familiar are you with the Book of Psalms? Can you identify some psalms that are particularly meaningful to you? Why are they?

2. Have you ever made much use of the psalms in your prayer or worship? How about in your church? Why or why not?

3. Can you see that a line is drawn, from the Old Testament through the New and all of Church history, of people who have used the psalms as God's program for their prayers and worship? What are the implications of this for believers and churches today?

4. What is your favorite psalm? Why? Is it the subject matter? The way it makes you feel? What it teaches about God? If you were to use this psalm as a kind of rudimentary prayer list, how might that prayer go? Take a few minutes and try praying through this psalm right now.

5. Given what we have seen in this chapter, how might you expect to benefit from beginning to make God's prayer program – the psalms – your own?

---

[1] John Calvin, *Geneva Psalter*, in Oliver Strunk, ed., *Source Readings in Music History*: The Renaissance (New York: W. W. Norton and Company, 1965), pp. 157, 158.

[2] The introductory material that follows can only be brief. For a fuller introduction to The Psalms, see Tremper Longman III, *How to Read the*

Psalms (Downers Grove: InterVarsity Press, 1988), or W. H. Bellinger, Jr., *Psalms: Reading and Studying the Book of Praises* (Peabody: Hendrickson Publishers, 1990).

[3] 1 Chronicles 15:16-24; 16:4-7.

[4] 1 Chronicles 26:1-19.

[5] 1 Chronicles 25:1-7; 15:19.

[6] John 5:39.

[7] 2 Samuel 22:6, cf. Psalm 116:3; 22:31, cf. Psalm 84:11.

[8] 1 Kings 8:36, cf. Psalm 25:4, 5; 2 Chronicles 6:40-42, cf. Psalm 132:8-10.

[9] 2 Kings 19:16, cf. Psalm 31:2; Daniel 2:20-24, cf. Psalm 103:1, 2.

[10] 2 Chronicles 29:30.

[11] Jonah 2:3, cf. Psalm 42:7; 2:9, cf. Psalm 3:8.

[12] I am grateful to my friend, Steven Wright, for much of the research for the following section.

[13] St Augustine, *Confessions*, R. S. Pine-Coffin, tr., (New York: Dorset Press, 1986), p. 191.

[14] A. Cleveland Coxe, ed., *Saint Augustin, Expositions on the Book of Psalms* (Peabody: Hendrickson Publishers, Inc., 1995), p. 186.

[15] "The Rule of Benedict" in Owen Chadwick, ed., Western Asceticism (Philadelphia: The Westminster Press, 1958), p. 309.

[16] Plummer, p. 46.

[17] "The Irish Life of Colum Cille", 22, in Maire Herbert, *Iona, Kells and Derry: The History and Hagiography of the Monastic Familia of Columba* (Dublin: Four Courts Press, 1996), p. 253.

[18] Quoted in William L. Holladay, *The Psalms through Three Thousand Years: Prayerbook of a Cloud of Witnesses* (Minneapolis: Fortress Press, 1993), p. 177.

[19] Leviticus 10.

3.

THE HEART OF THE PROGRAM

[The person who prays the psalms] will make the thoughts of the psalms his own. He will sing them no longer as verses composed by a prophet, but as born of his own prayers. At least he should use them as intended for his own mouth, and know that they were not fulfilled temporarily in the prophet's age and circumstances, but are being fulfilled in his daily life.

-Abba Issac[1]

Teach me your way, O LORD, that I may walk in your truth; unite my heart to fear your name. I give thanks to you, O Lord my God, with my whole heart, and I will glorify your name forever.

- Psalm 86.11, 12

Teach me how to pray using Your program, O God, for I do not know how to pray as I I ought. Then I will be walking in Your truth when I come to You in prayer; then my heart will truly fear You, as You call me to. Thank You, Lord my God, that You have given me these helps to prayer, and that you can teach me to use them. Let me do so with my whole heart, and I will glorify Your name forever.

God's prayer program begins with learning to pray the psalms. We come now to the heart of the matter. Convinced of the importance of prayer and of the value of using the psalms in that discipline, the question remains as to how we may do this. How can we learn to use God's prayer list to guide, strengthen, and compose our own prayers? After all, even a cursory glance at the psalms shows us that they are not all prayers, that is, not all addressed directly to God. They also seem, in many instances, to speak to or out of the context of situations and circumstances that seem only remotely connected to our own. And there are so many psalms, and some of them are so long. Where do we start?

In this chapter I want to introduce some ways of praying the psalms that can help us gain the most benefit from God's prayer program.[2] These are not so much individual ways of praying, however, as they are aspects of a single, overall approach to using the psalms in prayer. The six "methods" for or "approaches" to praying the psalms that I will discuss are rather like spokes on a wheel. As you are reading and experimenting with what follows, please try to keep this illustration of the wheel with six spokes in mind. In order for the wheel to do its work, all the spokes have to be in place and functioning properly. Though each spoke is separate, they all look rather alike, and they are all integral parts of the wheel as a whole. On a wheel, only one spoke in particular is required to bear the weight of the load at any given time, the one that is perpendicular to the ground; however, since the wheel is in constant motion, all the spokes must be strong and functioning, ready to serve as needed.

In the same way, the methods for or approaches to praying the psalms that I will share in this chapter are not intended for use with any particular psalm, or any particular type of psalm. Rather, those who want to pray the psalms should learn to use all these methods or approaches, and to use them freely and all together with any of the psalms, as the Lord leads in prayer. The objective is to be able to move from one approach – one spoke – to another as we work our way through a psalm, so that, ultimately, we should almost become unconscious of using any specific method of praying for any particular psalm, but should be able to pray as the Lord leads us, mastering all the methods for and approaches to praying the psalms and employing them freely and easily all together.

But before we discuss these different ways of praying the psalms, let's make sure we understand the overall goal of this undertaking.

THE GOAL OF PRAYING THE PSALMS

I don't think I could say it any better than did Abba Issac at the beginning of this chapter, or than Athanasius did in the fourth century:

> He who recites the psalms is uttering [them] in his own words, and each sings them as if they were written concerning him...[H]e handles them as if he is speaking about himself. And the things spoken are such that he lifts them up to God as himself acting and speaking them from himself.[3]

Simply put, the goal of learning to pray the psalms is to make the psalms our own prayers. We're not interested in promoting just another tedious devotional activity designed to enhance our sense of self-righteousness and enroll us in the ranks of modern

Pharisees. We want to be able to appropriate the words of the psalms as though they were our own words, to know and use those Spirit-given prayers as our own prayers, and to be carried along by them as we sail into the very presence of God with confidence and power. We want the themes of the psalms to be our themes, the affections they tap to be our affections, the very words they use to be our own words. Praying the psalms can be just like any other failed approach to prayer that you have ever tried. But it doesn't have to be. If you can learn to make the psalms your own, to enter into the words, moods, and subjects of these songs, hymns, prayers, and confessions of faith and make them your own in prayer before the Lord, you will be able to find the power and satisfaction in prayer that we all earnestly desire. This is the goal for learning to use the six ways of praying the psalms, as parts of an overall approach to adopting God's prayer program, that I will explain in this chapter.

Two secondary goals

Two secondary goals derive from this main goal.

(1) First, I want to encourage you to begin praying the psalms as a regular discipline. Plan to use all the psalms in your prayer, and to pray through the psalter on a regular basis, following a schedule that fits your needs. That's not to say that the psalms are the only thing you will pray, or that, whenever you pray, you must find some psalm to use. Not at all. However, I do wish to encourage you to establish

the practice of praying through the entire psalter on a regular, disciplined basis, so that you become increasingly familiar with all the psalms. Then you will gain the benefit in prayer that each of them has to offer. This will mean making some changes in your normal devotional practice, and I will suggest some ways that you can do this, both in this chapter and in chapters that follow, as well as in the appendices.

(2) Second, our goal is to have the psalms increasingly available to us whenever we pray, so that our prayers at the dinner table, with our families, in Bible studies, as we're driving in our cars – whenever – are informed and guided by the words and thoughts that are recorded in the psalms. Again, this can only serve to strengthen those prayers, to give us more confidence that all our prayers will be pleasing to God, and to provide us with words to use in coming before His throne of grace as often as we have opportunity or need. You will find that this goal begins to be unconsciously achieved as you work at mastering the six methods for praying the psalms in a regular, disciplined way. As your prayers become more filled and guided by the psalms, you will find that they affect others who are praying with you, just as that pastor's prayer using Psalm 30 profoundly affected everyone in that room. Your prayers, in other words, will be more of a blessing to you, as well as to those who join you in prayer, as you take up God's program of prayer and use the psalms with greater consistency.

Each of the methods I will be presenting has this much in common: They are all ways of allowing the psalms to guide, inform, and compose our prayers before the Lord. The differences between them are not dramatic; in some ways, these methods or approaches may look rather alike – like the spokes on a wheel. As I have said, these are not so much distinct approaches to praying the psalms as aspects of one overall approach to using God's prayer program. There are some subtle differences. but, as you learn to employ these approaches to praying the psalms, you will find that your sense of the differences dissolves, and your awareness of using one or another method evaporates, as the psalms become, increasingly, your own prayers before the glorious throne of grace.

A word of warning and encouragement
Before proceeding I should advise you that taking up the discipline of praying the psalms will not be easy. No true discipline ever is. Readers looking for an easier way to more vital and satisfying prayer will not find it in what follows – nor anywhere else. Prayer is hard work, and learning to the pray the psalms will be one of the most trying challenges you will ever take up. But take heart: saints throughout the ages have found this discipline to be a source of great power and satisfaction in prayer. You can, too.

Let's look, then, at the six ways of praying the psalms that can help you begin to find greater power and satisfaction in your prayers.

VERBATIM PRAYING

Some of the psalms lend themselves to what I call verbatim praying. That is, we can simply pray the words that are right there in the text, without any need to change, adapt, improve, add to, or interpret them. The psalm says exactly what we want to say, or what we need to say, and we can pray effectively using the words just as they are. We may feel led in places to add our own words, after we have prayed those of the psalmist; but, for the most part, we find the words of the psalm perfectly adequate for the purposes of our prayer.

While this way of praying the psalms is best suited for portions of many psalms, it can be employed with single psalms as well. Psalm 90, a psalm of Moses, provides a good example of this kind of praying. Here are the first three verses:

> Lord, you have been our dwelling place in all generations.
> Before the mountains were brought forth, or ever you had formed the earth and world, from everlasting to everlasting, you are God.

Take a few moments just now to pause and pray these words, just as you see them here.

In these verses Moses is simply acknowledging the eternality of the Lord and our own safe dwelling in Him, as well as His role as Creator of the world. Contained in that confession of faith is praise for God's adopting us as His people, for His faithfulness and unchanging nature. He is our God, and we are His people; this always has been, and always will be. He made us, and He shelters us within Himself in the world He has made. Pray these verses one more time, reflecting as you pray on their content, and how what they teach relates to you. When we understand the essential message of these verses, praying them verbatim will seem perfectly natural.

The psalm continues:

> You return men to dust and say, "Return, O children of man!" For a thousand years in your sight are but as yesterday when it is passed, or as a watch in the night. You sweep them away as with a flood; they are like a dream, like grass that is renewed in the morning: in the morning it flourishes and is renewed; in the evening it fades, and withers.

Pray these verses verbatim, reflecting on their meaning as you do.

In these verses Moses declares God's sovereignty over our lives. He is timeless, but we are finite. He rules over our lives sovereignly, as His pleasure dictates, and sees our whole lives as if in a moment of time. We are fleeting, and our days are in His hands. As we pray, these words will remind us both of the brevity of our lives – and, by implication, of the necessity of living them in full obedience to the Lord – and of the goodness of God Who cares enough to take note of our short lives. This theme occurs in several places in the psalms: who are we, insignificant creatures of dust, mere shadows, less than a breath, that God the Creator and sovereign Lord takes note of our lives? As you pray these verses again, meditate on the great privilege it is to be made in the image of God, and to have Him caring for you.

Further,

> For we are brought to an end by your anger, by your wrath we are dismayed. You have set our iniquities before you, our secret sins in the light of your presence. For all our days pass away under your wrath; we bring our years to an end like a sigh. The years of our life are seventy, or even by reason of strength, eighty: yet their span is but toil and trouble; they are soon gone, and we fly away.

Try praying all the first ten verses of this psalm aloud now. Praying aloud can add more reality to your prayers, and make them more meaningful. Take a moment and pray Psalm 90:1-10 aloud.

In verses 7-10 Moses leads us to admit our sinfulness and unworthiness before the Lord. Our sin in the presence of God's holiness is part of the reason we need to learn to fear the Lord. We deserve His anger, and in the face of His wrath, we are deeply troubled, especially when we consider that He knows even the secret sins that we have committed. The longer we live, the guiltier we become before Him, and, even though our lives are brief – 70 or 80 years – they are filled with trials and sorrows because of our sins. And then we die. This section of the psalm should have the effect of humbling us before the Lord, as we consider our sins in the light of His sovereign, eternal greatness. As we pray this psalm verbatim – try it once again to this point – we should feel our affections moving downward, from wonder and awe and high privilege to shame and fear.

But that's not the end:

> Who considers the power of your anger, and your wrath, according to the fear of you? So teach us to number our days, that we may get a heart of wisdom.

Pray this verse aloud. In fact, pray it over several times aloud.

Here Moses acknowledges our debt to God: In view of our sin and His just anger and wrath, we fear Him, reverence and honor Him, and plead with Him to show us how we ought to live, so that He will be pleased with our lives. Given His greatness and power, and the grace He has bestowed on us, both by making us and by being our dwelling place, we are not content to live our lives out in sin before Him. We want wisdom to make better use of our time, our days, our lives. Only as He guides us each day, as He teaches us how to "number our days", will we be able to know His wisdom and live in a manner that is pleasing to Him. I have this verse framed on a poster just to the left of the door of my study; it is the last thing I see as I head out in the morning for the day ahead. I pray these words every day, and, when I pray this psalm, I repeat this verse numerous times.

Moses continues, exposing his heart's desire to know the joy of the Lord:

> Return, O LORD! How long? Have pity on your servants! Satisfy us in the morning with your steadfast love, that we may rejoice and be glad all our days. Make us glad for as many days as you have afflicted us, and for as many years as we have seen evil.

Pray this verse and the last one aloud together.

The psalmist, seeking relief from the affliction caused by the knowledge of his sin and the brevity of his life, seeks the Lord's compassion, steadfast love, and joy. He seeks it because He knows this to be the character of God, and because He responds to us when we pray and seek His favor. Only as the Lord looks down on us with favor are we able to know peace and joy and make something out of our lives during the time God has been pleased to give us.

The last stanza suggests that this psalm is in many respects focused on Moses' work as a leader of God's people:

> Let your work be shown to your servants, and your glorious power to their children. Let the favor of the Lord our God be upon us, and establish the work of our hands upon us; yes, establish the work of our hands!

Just the kind of thing any of us might pray as we prepare for another day of serving the Lord in whatever our work might be. Take a moment to pray these words aloud.

Think about the message of this psalm, and its words as a focus of our prayers: Lord, You are my dwelling-place, my Maker, and my Redeemer. Show me what You want me to do today. Guide me in the way of wisdom. Do not hold my sins against me. Help me to make the best use of my time during these few years You have allotted to me. Cause my work to prosper. Let my children see Your majesty, and help us all to do that which is pleasing to You. All these thoughts are contained in these few verses, and, when we understand the message of this psalm, we can pray it word for word with confidence, meaning, and conviction.

Before going on in this chapter get your Bible, open to Psalm 90, and spend a few minutes praying this psalm verbatim back to the Lord. It will not take long, but if you will focus on the words, let yourself feel the affections, and sincerely express the requests the psalmist makes in this brief psalm, you'll experience something of the power and satisfaction that can come from making God's prayer program your own.

It should be obvious that to pray this or any other psalm verbatim requires that we have a good feel for what the psalm is about. This will come over time, with repeated use, study, and meditation. Verbatim praying is the easiest way to begin using the psalms as God's prayer list for our lives. As I mentioned, this method can be adapted to praying parts of almost all the psalms. Other entire psalms that lend themselves to this method are 38, 44, 51, 56, 57, 67, and 80. These might be a good place to start in learning how to use the psalms in prayer.

PARAPHRASE PRAYING

A second way to use the psalms in prayer is what I call paraphrase praying. This kind of praying is useful when the wording or circumstances of the psalm do not exactly fit our own, but they suggest something very similar which comes to mind as we read the psalm. The prayers that I have been using to begin the chapters of this book are examples of paraphrase praying. For another example, here is Psalm 59:1-4:

> Deliver me from my enemies, O my God; protect me from those who rise up against me; deliver me from those who work evil, and save me from bloodthirsty men. For behold, they lie in wait for my life; fierce men stir up strife against me. For no transgression or sin of my own, O LORD, for no fault of mine, they run and make ready. Awake, come to meet me, and see!

Most of us do not have enemies like this lying in the bushes waiting to attack and destroy us (although some of God's people, in other parts of the world, certainly do – more on this later). David had such enemies, however, and God gave him these words to use in seeking the Lord's protection against his foes. We do, however, have spiritual enemies lying constantly in wait to attack and trip us up, as Paul and Peter remind us.[4] And we do need the help and protection of the Lord in dealing with them – recognizing and resisting the temptations they bring against us, guarding against falling into step with the sinful lifestyles of our unsaved contemporaries, and so on. Thus, we might rephrase, or paraphrase, these verses as follows:

> Lord, I know there are spiritual enemies lying in wait for me today. Deliver me from those spiritual forces of wickedness in high places that seek to distract and destroy me every day. Keep my focus on high, on You and on my Lord Jesus. Help me to recognize the temptations that come against me every day; do not let me be overly

influenced by the sinful ways of others; help me to be on my guard against the devil, who I know is stalking about like a roaring lion, today as ever. Lord, rise to my defense as I seek to stand strong in the battle that is before me today, and keep me through every temptation and trial.

Take a look again at Psalm 59:1-4 above. As you read over it, try praying these words in a paraphrase, using words appropriate to your own experience and need.

Typically, when I am using this method, I will read over the section of the psalm that lends itself to paraphrasing, reading to myself the words just as they are written, then go back and pray the verses according to how I think I can use them in my own life.

Let's look at another example. Here is Psalm 18:4-6, a difficult psalm for most of us to identify with:

The cords of death encompassed me; the torrents of destruction assailed me; the cords of Sheol entangled me; the snares of death confronted me. In my distress I called upon the LORD; to my God I cried for help. From his temple he heard my voice, and my cry to him reached his ears.

When I pray this psalm, it serves as a reminder of God's grace in my salvation. I begin by reflecting on the superscription, which gives us the historical setting of the psalm, and prompts me to remember the circumstances in my own life when the Lord came to me with His saving grace. Then I begin with the first verses, by acknowledging the greatness of God in making me His own, and delivering me from all my enemies. In the light of the superscription, these verses lead me to think back on how lost I was at the time the Lord made Himself known to me, how confused and even frightened I felt much of the time. I remember how easily I might have been led into a life of sin and revelry, into a path of destruction and wastefulness. And I recall how, at that time, I would pray the Lord's prayer every night before I went to bed, not because I understood it, but because it was the only prayer I knew, and I somehow knew that prayer was a good thing. So when I pray these verses, here is how I might paraphrase them:

> Lord, when You came to me and rescued me, I was dead in my trespasses and sins. I was surrounded by ungodliness and tempted very strongly to go that way in my life. I was very close to stepping into hell's death-trap, and I was frightened and confused. All I could do was pray, even though I did not understand what I was praying. In Your grace and mercy You heard me; You sent messengers to declare the Good News of Jesus to me; and You heard me when I cried out in repentance and faith to You.

In paraphrase praying, as I have said, it is best to read through the part of the psalm you are going to pray, usually a stanza or so (conveniently divided for us in most English Bibles). Then spend a few moments meditating on the meaning of the verses you have read, especially how they might touch on some situation or need in your own life. Then, as you read back through them again, put them into words more appropriate to your own situation, letting the Spirit guide you by His inspired words as you bring your particular need or request before the Lord, using His outline and prompting. In my experience, this kind of praying can be useful in working through many of the psalms, as well as portions of most of them. You might try Psalms 9, 26, 36, 62, and 84.

I suppose just now I should offer a bit of a caveat. You are probably starting to get the idea that learning to pray the psalms, and actually using them in prayer, can take more time than you are accustomed to in prayer. You are correct. Remember the seventeen reasons for prayer we examined earlier. Recall that God commands us to pray. Reflect on the fact that He has given us the Book of Psalms to guide us in our prayers. *We must be prepared, in adopting God's prayer program, to devote more time to prayer*. Prayer is the most valuable thing we can do with our time. We will do with our time what we want to do, and nothing else. And, as you find that praying the psalms can be a source of great satisfaction and power, you will *want to find more time* for this glorious activity. So don't worry about that right now, about how you're going to find the time to adopt God's prayer program. I assure you, if you enter this program gradually, by beginning to pray the psalms a little each day, you will find all the time you want and need for prayer.

PRAYING OVER A PSALM

Somewhat similar to paraphrase praying is what I call praying over a psalm. I have found this method especially useful for praying longer psalms, especially those psalms which rehearse God's saving work for Israel or His sovereignty over the world (such as Psalms 78 and 105, or 104 and 147). In this method, being very familiar with the content of the psalm and the flow of its argument, I will not always read every word of the psalm, but will simply summarize large sections and try to apply them to my own circumstances as I do, praying as I scan my way through the psalm.

For example, Psalm 104 surveys the sovereign grace of God in providing for His creation. It begins with a declaration of His eternal majesty and splendor (vv. 1, 2), then moves to a proclamation of His work as Creator and Lord (vv. 3, 4). From there the psalm surveys God's providential sustenance of all He has made (vv. 5-30), ending with a paean of praise and a commitment to perpetual praise and rejoicing (vv. 31-35).

As I scan what has become for me a very familiar psalm I simply summarize in prayer the content or theme of each stanza, looking for cue words or phrases, and letting my prayer be guided by the psalm, but allowing it to go in whatever direction I may be inclined. For example, here is how I might pray over vv. 18-23:

> Lord, You have provided shelter for every one of Your creatures, including me. I thank You that, as You have given the mountains for wild goats, the hills for the rock badger, and places for every other creature, You have given me this home, with all its furnishings and blessings. I thank You for the different seasons of the year and the beauty each affords; for the day and the night, time to work and time to rest; and for a proper place for

everything in my life. Thank You for the work You've given me to do. Today in particular I ask you to help me with _____. Help me to be faithful in all my work, even as Your other creatures faithfully pursue the work You've called them to each day.

The main difference between this way of praying and paraphrase praying is that, being very familiar with the content of the psalm, I don't read each verse of the psalm (not always, anyway) but merely scan it, allowing the themes in a stanza of the psalm to prompt me to pray according to the subject they suggest. I am not so wedded to the actual words of individual verses, as I am inclined to be in paraphrase praying, as to the thoughts or themes of a particular stanza. Often, as I am praying over a psalm, my prayers will branch out into many related subject areas as the Spirit prompts my mind and blows me in new and exciting directions through the psalm.

Here is another example of this way of praying from Psalm 106:6-12:

Lord, we are sinners just like our fathers in the wilderness were. We are as wicked and evil as they were. Just as they so easily lost sight of all You did for them, so do we, so do I. Just as they forgot all your kindness toward them, so do we, so do I. Yet You saved them; You continued to support them; You showed Your grace to them in spite of the hardness of their hearts. You delivered them from all their enemies; You moved heaven and earth to deliver them to Yourself. They believed You then, and they sang Your praise. I praise You, too, Lord, for the way You delivered me from my sin and made me Your own dear child. I thank You for Jesus, for His perfect righteousness, saving death, and powerful resurrection. I thank You that He intercedes for me, and for all my loved ones, and all Your people, even now. Help me to remember Your kindness to me and never let me lose sight of all You have done for me.

I find it useful, from time to time, to read through these psalms that I typically pray over, just so I don't miss anything through familiarity. So, about every third or fourth time I come to one of these psalms, I will read it through a stanza at a time, then go back and pray over it as usual, or paraphrase pray it, incorporating any new themes or insights I might have gained. My ability to pray over these longer psalms is also helped by regular reading and study of the psalms as part of my normal Scripture reading schedule.

Responsive Praying

A fourth method I use for praying the psalms I call responsive praying. Here the psalm presents a theme, an idea, or a situation, although it is not itself in the form of a prayer. I read through the psalm a verse or stanza at a time, then pray it back to the Lord, responding to matters raised in the psalm, or as it otherwise guides me. Here is how I might pray Psalm 1 responsively, with the psalm in italics, and my prayer in normal type:

Blessed is the man who walks not in the counsel of the wicked, nor stands in the way of sinners, nor sits in the seat of scoffers; but his delight is in the law of the LORD, and in his law he meditates day and night.

Lord, I seek Your blessings for this day. Keep me from sin. Do not let me listen to sinful counsel. Keep my feet in the way of righteousness, and do not let me turn to or take up any sinful ways. Let no wicked practices settle in on me. Lord, help me to delight in Your Law, to read and study it with joy and relish, to think about it throughout the day, and to consider carefully its meaning for my life. Let what I have studied be with me all day today; let me meditate on it and let it be ready at hand when temptation comes to help me stay on Your path.

He is like a tree planted by streams of water, that yields its fruit in its season, and its leaf does not wither. In all that he does, he prospers.

Root me deeply in Your Word, O Lord, and let the river of Your grace and your Spirit water me afresh every day! Fill me with Your Spirit, Lord. Bring forth the fruit of righteousness in me, the fruit of the Spirit and the tokens of love, the fruit of powerful witness to You, and the fruit of holy living. Let me prosper in all that I seek to do for You, O Lord, including those responsibilities and opportunities that are before me today (here I might name some things on my daily schedule).

The wicked are not so, but are like chaff that the wind drives away. Therefore the wicked will not stand in the judgment, nor sinners in the congregation of the righteous...

Lord, this morning I think of those people I know who do not know You. I'm reminded of (here I will name the people in my personal mission field for whom I regularly pray and with whom I seek opportunities for witness. If they have particular needs, I will bring them to the Lord at this time. I will also pray for an opportunity to talk with one or more of them, especially ones I might see this day.). Lord, give them a sense of their responsibility to

You. Let Your Spirit strive with them. Make them mindful of Your judgment. Help them to seek You, so that they might become part of Your family as well.

...for the LORD knows the way of the righteous, but the way of the wicked will perish.

Lord, I know that the only reason You look on me as righteous is because of the work that Jesus has done for me. You have clothed me in His righteousness, and You are working out Your salvation in righteousness in me. Let that great work go forward and increase in me, and in all Your people, today. I know that You will watch over my way today, and I thank You for delivering me from eternal wrath. Let those who do not know You see something of You in me today, O Lord, and let that be a spark to turn them from wickedness to You.

Responsive praying thus establishes a dialog with God, in which, as He speaks from His Word, rather than paraphrasing what we have read, or scanning it for themes, we can respond to it in a manner appropriate to our circumstances or needs. It is for this reason that I find this to be one of the richest ways of praying the psalms. Many psalms lend themselves to this kind of praying, such as Psalms 37, 73, 87, 99, and 114.

GUIDED PRAYING

Another way to pray the psalms is what I call guided praying. In fact, you can use this method with any of the ones mentioned thus far. The distinctive of this method is that the psalm is actually guiding you to pray for something particularly pressing in your life or the life of someone else. The psalm presents a theme that is so clearly parallel to your own circumstances, or those of someone you know, that you let the verses of the psalm suggest a topic, then you go off in prayer for as many specific applications of that topic as the Lord is pleased to bring to mind at any particular time. A kind of combination of praying over a psalm and praying it responsively, this approach is unique in that it allows you, for example, to take up a particular list or theme in your prayers, and focus exclusively on that.

For example, Psalm 67 clearly lends itself to praying for missions. Here you can let the Spirit guide you to think about missions organizations, missionaries, your church's missions program, or your own involvement in missions. In my own work the men in one level of our Men's Discipleship Ministry are learning to sing and pray this psalm, keeping in mind as they do their need for the filling of God's Spirit to lead them to people who need to hear the Good News. So I use this psalm to guide me in praying for all the men who work with me in this ministry, and for those who, by learning to sing this psalm, will be reminded day by day of God's calling on our lives.

Psalm 129 deals with persecution. You can use it to pray for believers who are being persecuted for their faith, naming specific countries, situations, or people as the Lord brings them to mind. If you are not aware of any such situations, you should make this a matter of personal study. There are several sources for learning about the persecuted church.

Your pastor or missions committee can point you to some of them.

Psalm 47 envisions the Lord ruling over all the nations, and the princes of the nations becoming the people of Abraham. This psalm leads me to think of the Church's work in evangelism, calling the nations to believe the Gospel and submit to King Jesus. I pray for my own evangelism in my personal mission field, for the evangelistic outreach of our church, for churches in my community and around the world. I pray that God would re-kindle the fire of evangelism in us, that He would begin to work in the hearts of unbelievers and prepare them to hear the Gospel, and that He would bring a mighty harvest into His house. Typically, this psalm leads me into a general season of prayer for the Church's work of bearing witness to Christ, a work that has fallen on hard times of late, and is greatly in need of revival.

Psalm 72 leads in praying for our government officials, as well as (and especially) for the advance of Christ's Kingdom. Psalm 80 seeks revival in the Church. Psalm 73 deals with temptation. If our minds are engaged as we are praying the psalms we will find that they guide us to think of many specific needs, people, or situations in our lives and the lives of those we know and love. The Spirit can prompt us, bringing to mind the kinds of things He wants us to pray for on any given day, but we must be willing to be guided and to let the psalms do their work of suggesting items for prayer before the throne of grace.

ALTOGETHER NOW

The final method of praying the psalms is really a combination of all the above. As you begin to master the different ways of praying the psalms you will find that you can move easily from one method to another as you work your way through any particular psalm. This is the most frequent kind of praying the psalms that I do each day, as I allow the form, content, or theme of the psalm to suggest the best way of praying it. I may begin a psalm verbatim, such as in Psalm 18:1-3, then switch to paraphrase praying for vv. 4-15, a form of praying over the psalm for vv. 16-24, back to verbatim for vv. 25-29, to a responsive approach in vv. 30-45, and then verbatim praying to wrap it up (vv. 46-50). Normally I'm not conscious of making these switches. I'm sure that I never pray a psalm in the same way each time. It's just that, being familiar with how to use each method, and following carefully the form or content of the psalm, I can move back and forth with relative ease in what comes out as a fairly smooth and richly rewarding prayer.

As you get started praying the psalms, I suggest you find several that you can pray verbatim. Begin to do this right away. Then, as you begin to feel comfortable with those psalms, use them to begin practicing all the other methods I have described. From there you should be able to branch out to any of the psalms with relative ease. Be patient. Don't start off too large. Take your time, and let your delight grow in learning to use God's program for your prayers. The key is to begin, right away, to let God's prayer program lay down a foundation for all your prayers. How you can do that more effectively is the subject of our next chapter.

QUESTIONS FOR STUDY OR DISCUSSION

1. In this chapter you were asked to do various things in praying the psalms. Did you do them? What was your experience as you did?

2. Using the psalm that you indicated at the end of the last chapter as your favorite, for the next half-hour or so, try praying that psalm, practicing as many of the approaches discussed in this chapter as you can. Which seem to work best for you?

3. If you could select seven psalms – one for each day of the week – to begin learning to pray in the ways discussed in this chapter, what would they be? Beginning in the morning, but taking time also during the day and before you go to bed, try praying those psalms, one per day, using various of the methods we have examined. Share your experience of doing this with another person.

4. As you begin to think about, and actually start, using God's prayer program – praying the psalms – what frustrations, doubts, or concerns do you have? How will you deal with these?

5. Review the goals you set for this study of God's prayer program. Are you reaching them? In what ways? Do you need to revise or add to them in any ways?

[1] Owen Chadwick, ed., *Western Asceticism* (Philadelphia: The Westminster Press, 1958), pp. 243, 244.

[2] An earlier and condensed version of this chapter may be found in the introduction to *The Psalms for Prayer* (Grand Rapids: Baker, 2002).

[3] Athanasius, *The Life of Antony and the Letter to Marcellinus*, trans. Robert C. Gregg (New York: Paulist Press, 1980), p. 10.

[4] Ephesians 6:10-20; 1 Peter 5:8.

4.

GETTING WITH THE PROGRAM

Apart from their connection with the liturgical year and their ability to draw us into the mind of Christ, the psalms, written under the inspiration of the Holy Spirit, in themselves have power to lead us to God. They give voice to the cries of the human heart: to joy, pain, frustration and grief. Exposure to the broad spectrum of the psalms as they are prayed daily over the course of life, builds up in us a treasury of words for our own prayers.

- Sister Janet Baxendale[1]

But I call to God, and the LORD will save me. Evening and morning and at noon I utter my complaint and moan, and he hears my voice.

- Psalm 55:16, 17

Hear my prayer, O Lord; O my God, let my prayer come before You this day. I come in the morning; I will meet you at mid-day; and again this evening I will pray and plead, and cry out to You, persisting and persevering in Your grace, and You will hear me each time I pray.

I remember an old Steve Martin routine which he called, "How to Become a Millionaire." The first step is, as he inimitably put it, "Get a million dollars."

Taking up God's prayer program can be a little like that. You want to pray the psalms and enjoy all the satisfaction that comes thereby? First, pray the psalms. The problem, of course, is that the psalms are not all prayers; nor are they all directly addressed to our present circumstances, or in language that is always easy to grasp; plus, they are filled with allusions, historical referents, and other details that seem strangely out of place in the prayers of contemporary Christians. Many of the psalms seem strangely harsh, while others don't fit our moods or needs. We can see how some of the psalms might be workable for prayer, but all?

For many people, just jumping in to start praying the psalms can be about as easy as coming up with a million dollars! So even though we may be equipped with six different ways of approaching this discipline, we can still find the going rather rough and the goal disappointingly elusive, especially at the beginning.

The purpose of this chapter is to further outline the program for prayer God sets forth for us in the psalms and the rest of His Word, and to provide encouragement and guidance to you as you take up this wonderful but challenging discipline. I want to provide some guidelines and to highlight some particular challenges that you can expect to face as you begin to pray the psalms, in order to equip you to anticipate and overcome potential obstacles and get the most out of God's prayer program. We'll look first at some practical suggestions for personalizing the psalms in prayer, for making the words of the psalms more immediately your own and, thus, overcoming one of the primary obstacles that can keep you from using God's prayer list. Next we'll pay special attention to the matter of how to pray those psalms which are more overtly Messianic. After that I'll make some suggestions about how to find the time for praying through the entire psalter on a regular basis. Finally, we'll consider the challenges that arise from praying a few specific psalms, unique because they almost defy us to include them in our discipline. Our objective here, building on the preceding chapter, is to enable the reader to accomplish the goal that Colman of Ela enunciates in the following quote. When we're praying the psalms we should try to

> Speak in thine own character exactly,
> And fix on them thine understanding;
> Then thou shalt receive thy request from
> The King of the stars,
> Whose protection is never-ending.[2]

THE LANGUAGE OF THE PSALMS

We look first at Colman's challenge to personalize the psalms, to make their language our own. Six practical suggestions will help to get you through some of the anachronisms, unfamiliar allusions, and other potential stumbling-blocks to using God's prayer list so that you can make the psalms a more personal tool for your prayers.

Change the nouns and pronouns

The first relates to a simple change in nouns and pronouns. Many of the psalms speak of God in the third Person, as "God", "Lord", "the Almighty", "He", and so on. If we keep this language in every case as we pray through the psalms, it will seem strange to be praying to God and to be talking about Him rather than directly to Him.

The simple remedy for this little obstacle is to change all third-person references to God to the second person – "You" or "Your." Here is an example from the beloved Psalm 23, used in a paraphrase-praying mode:

> The LORD is my shepherd;
> I shall not want.
> He makes me lie down in green pastures;
> He leads me beside still waters.
> He restores my soul.
> He leads me in the paths of righteousness
> For his name's sake.

> Lord, You are my shepherd;
> I have all that I need.
> You fill my life with every abundant blessing;
> You bring me perfect peace and daily refreshment.
> You renew my soul every day;
> You show me how to live according to Your holy Word
> So that I will glorify You.

Another example may be helpful. Here are the first two verses of Psalm 76, again in paraphrase-praying:

> In Judah God is known;
> his name is great in Israel.
> His abode has been established in Salem,
> his dwelling place in Zion.

> Lord, Your people know You well;
> We exalt Your name, O Lord.
> You have come to dwell among us by Your Spirit;
> I know that You live in my heart, as
> You do in all those who know You.

We should make every effort to personalize the psalm by expressing it as our own prayer, and turning third-person references to second-person ones can help us. This way we're using the words that God has provided in order to speak directly to Him and not just about Him.

Related to this, we may find at times that psalms involving first person plural pronouns ("we") can be just as easily used to express our singular concerns, and the other way around as well. Matters that the psalms address in the singular may well apply to others besides us – our families, churches, or communities. We can easily change these references and thus make the psalms more relevant to our own situations or needs.

Interpret Old Testament references in New Testament categories

In the example of Psalm 76 we encounter a second kind of obstacle. That is the many references in the psalms to Israel and to events and places connected with the redemptive work of God in the Old Testament. What do we do about these?

Here we may allow all Old Covenant images – Zion, Israel, the land, burnt offerings, and so forth – to represent New Covenant realities, following principles of interpretation set forth in the New Testament itself. We can especially see this illustrated in a passage like Hebrews 12:22-24:

> But you have come to Mount Zion and to the city of the living God, the heavenly Jerusalem, and to innumerable angels in festal gathering, and to the assembly of the first-

born who are enrolled in heaven, and to God, the judge of all, and to the spirits of the righteous made perfect, and to Jesus, the mediator of a new covenant, and to the sprinkled blood, that speaks a better word than the blood of Abel.

Here the writer equates Zion with the Church ("assembly") and shows that Christ is the fulfillment of the Old Testament sacrifices. When we encounter references to Israel, therefore, we may apply them to ourselves as members of the Body of Christ and the people of God today. Other passages that teach us so to interpret such Old Testament images are Matthew 5:13-16 (cf. Micah 4:1-5) and 1 Peter 2:9, 10 (cf. Hosea 1:6, 9, 10). Declarations that we intend to offer our sacrifices up to God can lead us to think not only of Jesus' sacrifice, which we claim anew for ourselves, but also of the sacrifices of praise and thanksgiving with which God is most pleased, as well as our own lives as living sacrifices of righteousness unto the Lord.[3] References to the deliverance from Egypt can lead us to think about our own deliverance salvation. The subduing of the land and the promises it represents can call to mind the progress of the Church on earth and of our own sanctification, and the fuller realization of the promises of God. References to Israel's kings and judges can prompt us to pray for our own rulers, civil and ecclesiastical. I have always found that those ancient images become particularly fresh and relevant when translated into New Covenant terms and personally applied, such as in this example of praying-over Psalm 81:6, 7:

Lord, You relieved me from the burden of sin and set me free from my slavery to unrighteous works and thoughts. When I call upon You, as I do each day, You come to my aid; You answer my prayers from Your holy, majestic throne; You have often tried me in order to test and grow my faith, and I thank You. Do not let me despise Your testings and discipline, but help me to receive them and be corrected by them, always keeping in mind the grace You have shown in saving me.

In this example as well the reader will see that I have made another shift in person, from God speaking to me, as He speaks to Israel in these verses, to reciting His words back to Him, at the same time that I am making the adjustment for my own circumstances, based on what God accomplished for Israel when He delivered them from Egypt. So I am praying responsively and praying-over these verses at the same time.

Keep the spiritual warfare in mind

Third, many of the psalms involve David or another psalmist praying for God's protection against or vindication from his enemies. These are imprecatory psalms, or psalms of imprecation. We may find praying these psalms a little difficult, since we do not find ourselves threatened by many enemies, at least not in the West, and since some of them involve some pretty harsh language.

There are two ways to use these parts of God's prayer list with benefit.

(1) The first is to apply these psalms to our spiritual warfare. All who follow Christ are constantly engaged

in a great spiritual warfare with powerful spiritual adversaries who want nothing so much as to distract, discourage, and defeat us in our walk with the Lord.[4] We are called to resist their ploys and attacks so that we may share in Christ's triumph over His foes and ours.[5] Prayer can be an effective means of overcoming in this spiritual warfare, as Jesus showed us in preparing for His own temptation.[6] When we come to a psalm like Psalm 3, we can easily apply it to our struggle with spiritual forces of wickedness in high places:

> O Lord, how my adversaries have increased, those spiritual forces of wickedness that are seeking to destroy me! Every day they rise up against me, tempting me to think that I'll never grow in my faith, never get rid of the sin that continues to defeat me, never know more of Your amazing saving grace. They only want to discourage, distract, and defeat me, Lord. But You protect me from them, Lord…

Some of these psalms can get downright vicious at times, such as Psalm 137. But remember, God is ultimately going to consign all His spiritual adversaries to the lake of fire and everlasting torment.[7] This is where they belong because of their determined and persistent rebellion against God, in spite of His grace and favor. Surely there can be nothing wrong with our imploring the Lord, using His own words, to "rough them up" a bit in the here and now for the sake of our sanctification, and to hasten the day when they will be dealt with once and for all.

110

(2) The second way to use these psalms is to remember that, while we in the West may not know the wrath of human enemies, plenty of our brothers and sisters in Christ throughout the world do, every day of their lives.[8] We may use these psalms, which call upon the Lord to overthrow His enemies, in defense of our persecuted brethren. My usual practice in this regard is to let all such prayers be tempered by Psalm 83:16, in which the prayer for God to strike back against the enemies of His people includes the petition that those enemies might come to their senses and begin to seek Him. We must always bear in mind that we are called to love our enemies and to pray for those who persecute us.[9] We'll be safest and most effective in those prayers if we use the words that God Himself has provided.

Letting the psalms bring others to mind
A fourth obstacle to using God's prayer list arises when we encounter psalms that do not describe our situation. Psalm 88 is the best example of this. Certain of the psalms send us to the depths of despair, only to rescue us through praise and refocusing on the Lord by the end, such as Psalm 43. Not Psalm 88. It starts depressed and gets worse, all the way to the end. Few of us ever feel this way (although we certainly may at times). But the Lord Jesus certainly did, as He prepared to bear our sins on the cross.[10] My practice in using this psalm, as well as any others that describe emotions or situations that don't fit me at the time, is to remember that, while I may not feel this way,

there are plenty of my fellow believers who do. Some of them I may know, including the details of their suffering. Others will be completely unknown to me. I can pray for them using these psalms and have the sense that I am bearing their burdens, even though I may not know them or the nature of their struggle. This psalm, and others involving suffering, can also lead us to praise and thank the Lord for what Jesus endured for us.

Praying for what God desires, or what He warns about

Fifth, there are some psalms that speak of situations that do not appear to be true at this time. This can make it a little confusing trying to pray them. Psalm 48, for example, describes the Church as "the joy of the whole earth." This seems hardly to be the case in our world that appears increasingly indifferent or even hostile to the Christian faith. Psalm 79 envisions the temple of God in ruins and His city (Church) overrun by heathen. Such psalms as this can be understood as describing either a situation that God desires to see, or one that we should be warned against. We may ask the Lord, following Psalm 48, for example, to revive His Church and bring about the kind of love, truth, and unity in her throughout the world that will cause the nations to see His glory in our midst and believe that the Father has sent His Son as Savior to the world.[11] Or, following Psalm 79, we can pray that God will deliver His Church from the influences of worldliness – substituting humanists, evolutionists, materialists, and other worldly influences for the nations mentioned there – that threaten to infiltrate our worship and our lives and undermine our distinctiveness in the world.

Sing the psalms

One final suggestion for overcoming obstacles of language and becoming more familiar and at ease with using the psalms is to sing them. A number of psalters, or, versifications of the psalms with music, are available.[12] Several benefits can come from singing the psalms. (1) First, we learn their content more readily and they tend to stay with us longer. Most people have little difficulty, after a few exposures, learning new songs, whether they have good singing voices or not (remember, all that the Lord requires is "a joyful noise"!). When those songs are the psalms, used as part of our daily devotions, and at other times throughout the day, we will learn them more easily and they will be more readily available to us at other times during the day for use in praising God and recalling all His benefits to us.

(2) Second, singing the psalms helps us to appreciate their affective value. All the psalms involve our emotions, appealing to our affections as well as our minds in order to engage us more fully with the Lord in prayer. Music seems to have a special ability to draw out our emotions, and this can help us to appreciate more fully the unique character of the psalms that we are using in prayer.

(3) Third, singing the psalms makes it easier to encourage our children to take up this discipline. As they hear us singing they will want to join in, and, as they do, they will begin to develop the discipline of using God's prayer list right along with us.

(4) Fourth, singing the psalms fulfills a direct command that we sing new songs to the Lord. Nothing restricts us to singing only when we are together in times of worship. Christians are called to sing always. Indeed, it is a mark of those who are filled with the Spirit of God that they sing to themselves and sing to one another![13]

(5) Finally, learning to sing the psalms equips us with a tool we can use throughout the day to bear witness to our faith in the living God and to praise Him before all people. As we sing to ourselves at work, in our homes, or as we are driving with others, God uses our songs to sow the Word of truth into the lives of others, whether or not they know Him.

In an appendix I have included some samples of psalms set to familiar tunes for singing. I recommend you try this and see if it doesn't help the psalms become more powerful as part of your discipline of prayer.

As you begin getting with God's prayer program for your daily prayers you will encounter various obstacles in the language of the psalms that might discourage you in your desire to employ this discipline. The suggestions in this section can help you to press on and overcome those obstacles so that you gain all the benefit in prayer God intends for us from his psalms.

PRAYING MESSIANIC PSALMS

Some time ago I participated in an examination of a young man who was seeking to be ordained to the Gospel ministry. These can be fairly trying occasions, and this particular young man had known his share of miscues along the way. It would be generous to say that the examination of his knowledge of the English Bible was not going all that well. At one point in the exam he was asked by one of the examiners how many Messianic psalms there are in the psalter. Without hesitation he replied, "One hundred and fifty," and immediately won the hearts of all present. His spirit was renewed, and he sailed through the rest of his exam without problems.

All the psalms, as well as all the rest of Scripture,[14] testify of our Lord Jesus Christ. He is the consistent, organizing theme of the whole Bible, the centerpiece of all God's redemptive work on behalf of His people. But the psalms include many that seem particularly pointed at Him in one way or another. Psalms 22 and 69, for example, can only be fully appreciated in the light of what they prophesy concerning Jesus' suffering and His work of atonement. Psalm 16, as Peter noted,[15] concerns the resurrection of our Lord. Psalm 109, as well as parts of other psalms, speaks to the betrayal of Christ. Psalm 110 portrays His exalted rule and the advance of His Kingdom. In addition, parts of many other psalms only make sense when they are prayed in the light of Christ's person or work, such as Psalm 18:20-24, in which the psalmist boasts of his (which is really Christ's) righteousness. How do we pray such psalms as these?

Keep in mind our union with Christ

First, keep in mind that it is only because of our union with Christ that we can come before the Lord in prayer at all.[16] Thus, Christ should never be very far away from our minds as we are praying any of the psalms. He is the reason we can seek forgiveness from the Lord for our sins (Psalms 32, 38, 51). He provides the righteousness with which we may come before the Lord in prayer (Psalms 1, 15, 18:20-24). He is our Shepherd, Guide, and Source of life-transforming power (Psalms 23, 25, 46, 78). Praise and thanks to Jesus should figure into every one of our psalms as we use these words from which He is never very far removed in our prayers before the Lord.

Recall the work of Christ

But in those psalms that are specifically devoted to Him it is well for us to linger long in recalling with praise and thanksgiving His work for our salvation. As we reflect, for example, on the various sufferings of Christ related in Psalm 22 – His loneliness, humiliation, fear, and torment – we will be led to thank Him in tears for bearing our sins in His own body on the cross, and for setting an example of trusting the Lord that we may learn to emulate. As we review the results of His atoning work from Psalm 69 – paying our debt, bearing our reproach, overcoming our enemies – we may joyfully share in the triumph of His death and resurrection, letting our hearts fill up with gladness because of His grace. Or as we reflect on His constant companionship and care as our Shepherd (Psalm 23) we will grow stronger in our confidence in and love for Him.

Meditate on His glory

Finally, we may use several of the psalms to meditate on Christ in His exalted state of glory, and to pray for the work He is doing now of advancing His Kingdom on earth, as it is in heaven. Psalms 45 and 68 invite us to peer into His throne room and wonder at the beauty of His majesty. Psalms 2 and 110 lead us to pray for His work of claiming the nations. Psalms 47 and 147 lead us in celebrating His work of calling out His elect and building His Church. And so on.

There is not a single aspect of the work of Christ that is not touched on at some point in the psalms. Thus, praying through them on a regular basis can help us to recall and celebrate all His glorious and powerful work on our behalf, enabling us increasingly to give Him the praise and honor which are due Him, and helping us to grow in love for Him each day.

FINDING TIME TO PRAY THE PSALMS

As a new Christian I remember being confronted by the man who was helping me to get started in my walk with the Lord about why I had not yet begun to develop a more consistent time in prayer and study of God's Word. I was a busy college student-athlete at the time, and so I figured I had a good reason. I said I simply did not have the time. He responded, "It's not that you don't have the time; you don't have the desire." I got a little defensive and said, "What Christian doesn't want to have a really good devotional time with the Lord?" To which he replied, "You!" He went on to say, "T. M., it's not a question of having enough time. We have just as much time as anyone else, and just as much time as the Lord thought we would need. Your problem is desire. We will do in our lives only and exactly what we want to do, nothing more. When you really want to have a meaningful discipline of Bible study and prayer, you will."

He was right, and I've never forgotten his advice. The key to having the time needed to get with God's prayer program is to want to. If we want to, that is, if we believe that it is so important and can mean so much for our growth in the Lord and our love for Him that we simply must do it – when we get to this point, we'll find we have all the time we need to pray the psalms according to God's prayer program on a regular basis.

Praying at set times

On the other hand, like anything else we do, having a schedule, or establishing set times for prayer, can help. The Scriptures themselves, as well as the example of our Christian forebears, give us some guidance here. David, for example, said that he would pray and praise God three times a day, "evening and morning and at noon."[17] Another of the psalmists (perhaps David, although that isn't clear), declared, "Seven times a day I praise You."[18] Should we take these words seriously?

It is apparent that Daniel did. In Daniel 6:10 we find the great prophet "kneeling on his knees three times a day, praying and giving thanks to the Lord." He was undoubtedly not alone among the Old Testament saints who knew the value of having set times during the day to draw aside for prayer. Daniel, as we know, was a very busy man in a not-so-friendly environment. But he was so consistent, so predictable in this discipline of praying three times a day, that his enemies knew exactly where to find him and what he would be doing when they wanted to charge him with the crime of praying at a time other than had been royally approved.

The Apostles in the New Testament also recognized something like these "hours of prayer." In Acts 3:1 we find Peter and John "going up to the temple at the hour of prayer, the ninth hour" that is, about 3:00 in the afternoon. Similarly, Peter, in Acts 10:9, retired to the rooftop of a home for his noontime hour of prayer.

This practice of establishing set hours of prayer, spread throughout the day, was carried over into the early and medieval Church, as our forebears in the faith followed the pattern of their (and our) Biblical fathers. James F. White, in his *Documents of Christian Worship*, provides a complete listing of Biblical and historical references to the practice of the hours of prayer, including a helpful chart.[19] A careful reading of the material in this section of his book will show the Biblical foundations and practical reasons why the first Christians felt this discipline to be so important to their lives in Christ.

Among certain segments of the Christian community, notably Roman Catholic religious, this discipline has never been set aside. For most of us, though, keeping the hours of prayer is an unknown discipline.

Why do we no longer hold to this practice? I can think of two reasons: (1) First, we are not as prayerful a people as our forebears. Because we live in times of ease and prosperity and have learned so much about the use of technique and technology in our walk of faith, we have less of a sense of dependence on the Lord than they did. In short, we don't pray as much as we should because we don't feel a need for it; we trust ourselves, our methods, and our prosperity more than we do the Lord.

(2) Second, however, I suspect many will say it is just not practical to keep the hours of prayer. There is just too much to do in a day. Too many appointments to keep. Too much business to do. All those errands, responsibilities, and things to do.

We just don't have the time.

Which is to say, *prayer is just not as great a priority as our other commitments.* The sooner we admit that this is the situation, the greater is the likelihood we will be able to overcome the time obstacle.

J. B. Philips, in his translation of Romans 12:1, 2, warned against letting the world "squeeze you into its mold." In the use of our time for prayer it seems we have allowed precisely this to happen. Our daily agendas are set more by the times in which we live than the priority of prayer and the example of our forebears in the faith. Here is an area where the followers of Christ need to redeem the time,[20] taking back valuable minutes from their mundane routines to invest in the work of prayer. We may protest that we're just too busy to keep set times of prayer during the day. Shall we try that excuse on a busy administrator like Daniel, or an on-the-move apostle like Paul? We might fear what others would think of us if we are always having to excuse ourselves for a few moments of prayer at different times during the day. But the fear of man, Solomon tells us, is a snare.[21] We may find it difficult to adjust our schedules to accommodate this practice, but that will only be at first. As we commit to frequent and regular times of prayer throughout the day, and as we devote ourselves to keeping this discipline, we will find that the Lord will honor this commitment and will make our practice increasingly a glorious retreat of worship and prayer.

Aim small, miss small

I love the scene in the film, *The Patriot*, in which Mel Gibson and his sons are getting ready to attack the enemy platoon that has taken their son and brother captive. Gibson wants his sons to do well, so he tells them to remember what he has taught them about shooting: "Aim small, miss small." The danger in beginning to think about setting times during the day to pray the psalms is that we try to do it all at once. We aim big – seven times a day, right out of the shoot! If we aim this big to begin with, we will not succeed in redeeming our time for prayer in this way.

Start small. Add one additional time for prayer a day for a number of weeks. Perhaps you will add some time for prayer just before the noon hour, or just after. Or maybe in mid-morning, or mid-afternoon. Put it on your calendar or appointment book, and treat it as you would any other appointment. If you work in a place where you cannot be alone, then let your prayers at such times be like Nehemiah's, who managed to pray to God (silently, it seems) in the midst of a conversation with the king![22] But start small. That way, if you miss your appointment for the day, you won't feel such a sense of utter defeat and frustration. You can always make a new appointment with the Lord for tomorrow.

Schedule time for each psalm

In due course you will get to the place where you will be able to carve out more time for prayer. You will do this because you will want to do this, not because you feel you have to. As you do, use at least some of that time to begin praying through all the psalms on a regular basis. For this, you will need a plan, or a schedule.

In an appendix I have included three schedules for praying through the psalter on a regular basis. You will notice that they are set up for you to be able to pray different psalms at different times of the day. For many years I have taught students to practice this discipline, and they have always found it to be a refreshing addition to their prayers. Recently I preached at the ordination service of a young man who was a student of mine for a number of years. At one point in the service another member of the ordaining commission, a minister who had also been a mentor to this young man, pulled out a well-marked, well-worn sheet of paper with a chart on it. He asked the congregation, where this young man had been serving as an interim pastor for a number of months, "Do you recognize this?" There was a laughter of recognition, as the congregation delighted in this man's flourishing the chart for praying through the psalms on a monthly basis, using the schedule my student had developed when he studied with me. The congregation not only recognized the chart, but many of them had begun to use it in their prayers as well.

PRAYING "PROBLEM" PSALMS

Some of the psalms almost defy us to pray them. Like Psalm 119. How is it possible to pray through these 176 verses without becoming distracted or hopelessly frustrated? One approach is to break the psalm down into segments. Since this is a psalm that deals exclusively with the Word of God, praying one of its 22 sections prior to one's daily devotions can be a very healthy way of beginning the reading and study of Scripture each day.

Psalm 45 is a particularly challenging psalm as well, especially after verse 9. What are we to make of these references to the "king's daughter", and, more importantly, how shall we pray them? My approach is to think of God as the King and the Bride of His

Son – the Church – as His daughter. Then I simply apply the teaching in a relevant way to the Church, and more particularly, myself.

Psalm 49 addresses the peoples of the world, warning them of the foolishness of unbelief. My usual approach is to pray that God would begin to convict the nations under the witness of His people to turn from their various idolatries and to trust in Him.

Similarly, Psalm 58 speaks to unrighteous "gods", or, world rulers. I use this psalm to remind myself of the futility of trusting political leaders or other worldly people who do not believe in the Lord. Then I pray for them that their eyes may be opened to see the truth of God.

These are just a few of the "problem" psalms that can confuse or discourage us in our effort to use God's prayer list on a regular basis. As you become more familiar with these psalms, and with their content and purpose, the Lord will show you ways to profit from them in prayer. Press on in praying them the best you can, and God will reward your faithfulness.

By now you should be getting the idea that the only real obstacle to praying the psalms on a regular basis and gaining the benefit they have for us is our own desire to do so. Once we come to believe in the value of this discipline and begin to get some practice doing it, the rewards – in satisfying, confident, powerful, and joyful prayer – will be sufficient to keep us going. So don't wait; get with God's prayer program right now, beginning wherever you can.

After all, this program holds great promise for your relationship with the Lord.

QUESTIONS FOR STUDY OR DISCUSSION

1. What other potential obstacles to praying the psalms can you imagine? How might you overcome those obstacles?

2. From what you have read thus far, do you find that you are beginning to want to use the psalms in prayer? Why or why not?

3. Turn to Appendix 2 at the end of this book and try singing through some of the examples of psalms set to familiar tunes. Sing them more than once. Can you see how doing this might be a valuable experience?

4. Is there someone you know who might encourage you and hold you accountable for praying the psalms? Meet with that person; tell him or her what you are studying and planning, and ask for help in carrying through with your plan. Meet from time to time to share what you are learning and to talk about ways you feel your prayers are improving.

5. Review the psalm you chose as your favorite at the end of chapter 2. Set a time other than your normal devotional time to pray this psalm each day for the next two weeks, practicing all the ways of praying the psalms we have discussed. At the end of those two weeks, reflect on your experience.

---

[1] Sister Janet Baxendale, "Spiritual Potential of the Liturgy of the Hours," in *Origins*, November 11, 1993, Vol. 23, No. 22, p. 389.

[2] In Plummer, p. 164.

[3] Psalm 50:14; Hebrews 13:15; Romans 12:1, 2; Psalm 4:5.

[4] Ephesians 6:12, 13; 1 Peter 5:8.

[5] 1 Peter 5:9; James 4:7.

[6] Matthew 4:1-11.

[7] Revelation 19:20.

[8] I might recommend a subscription to "Touchstone" magazine for those seeking information about the persecuted Church. Each issue carries a report on ways that our brethren are coming under attack in other parts of the world. The address is Touchstone, The Fellowship of St James, P. O. Box 410788, Chicago, IL 60641. Phone: 773-481-1090.

[9] Matthew 5:44; Luke 6:28.

[10] I am indebted to my father-in-law, Lane Adams, for first pointing this out to me.

[11] John 17:21.

[12] One example is *The Trinity Psalter* (Pittsburgh: Crown and Covenant Publications, 1994). See Appendix 2 for other samples of psalms set for singing.

[13] Ephesians 5:18-21.

[14] John 5:39.

[15] Acts 2:24-31.

[16] Hebrews 4:14-16.

[17] Psalm 55:17.

[18] Psalm 119:164.

[19] James F. White, *Documents of Christian Worship* (Louisville: Westminster/John Knox Press, 1992), pp. 75-91.

[20] Ephesians 5:16.

[21] Proverbs 29:25.

[22] Nehemiah 2:4.

5.

THE PROMISE OF THE PROGRAM

If we wish to develop in the life of faith, to mature in our humanity, and to glorify God with our entire heart, mind, soul, and strength, the Psalms are necessary. We cannot bypass the Psalms. They are God's gift to train us in prayer that is comprehensive (not patched together from emotional fragments scattered around that we chance upon) and honest (not a series of more or less sincere verbal poses that we think might please our Lord)...If we are willfully ignorant of the Psalms, we are not thereby excluded from praying, but we will have to hack our way through formidable country by trial and error and with inferior tools.

-Eugene H. Peterson[1]

One thing I have asked of the LORD, that I will seek after: that I may dwell in the house of the LORD all the days of my life, to gaze upon the beauty of the LORD and to inquire in his temple.

- Psalm 27:4

Lord, what do I want? What am I seeking from You as I come to You in prayer? This, and this only: to be ever in Your presence, in the midst of Your glory; to see You in all Your beauty; and to bring my requests before Your glorious throne.

Imagine that you are three years beyond this moment. Your family is a little older, your job a little more demanding. Perhaps you have a new car, or have made some new addition to your home. Maybe you've put on a little weight – or taken some off! Your old friends are still a vital part of your life, and you've made some new ones. The old cares and worries are still hanging around, and perhaps a few new ones have made their presence felt as well; but, on the whole, you see yourself happier, more content, and at greater peace with yourself and the world. All in all, like most of us, you probably imagine your life getting better – more satisfaction from your work, more time with the family, a better relationship with your spouse, a few more of the things that make life happier and better. Most of us do, which is why we continue to pursue the tack we have chosen to sail each day: We are convinced that this is the way of happiness for us.

But what about your life spiritually? Three years from now, will you be stronger in the Lord? More able to resist temptation? More consistently filled with His joy and peace? A readier witness for Him? Better able to show His love to every person you meet? More in tune with His calling for your life, His unique purpose and plan for you? Will you have a greater hunger for His Word, and a more intense desire to follow Him in every area of your life? Will you delight in Him as much as He delights in you, and will you seek and enjoy His presence as often and as abundantly as He desires for you? Will you know the presence and beauty of the Lord more personally, more consistently, and more powerfully every day?

I suspect that most of us do not think of our lives spiritually in the same way that we do the other areas of our lives. For most of us, our attitude toward growing spiritually is que será será: We set no goals, give our spiritual future little thought, and, in comparison with the rest of our lives, exert ourselves hardly at all to attain a fuller, more powerful and meaningful spiritual life. Whatever will be, will be. We may have adopted certain spiritual routines that we hope will help us to maintain some modicum of growth and spiritual vitality; yet, for the most part, we have no vision of a more vital and growing spiritual future. Perhaps if we did, and if we found that vision truly compelling, we might exert ourselves rather more diligently in the use of such spiritual disciplines as prayer.

In this chapter I want to hold out for you a vision of what you might reasonably expect to happen in your life over the next several years if you were to give yourself faithfully and diligently to following God's prayer program as the foundation of your prayers. It is my own experience, and that of many others, that praying the psalms can contribute mightily to having a stronger and more vital spiritual life. Especially in three areas you can expect to see dramatic changes: The role of prayer in your life, your vision of unseen things, and your relationship with the Lord. The growth that you can expect to know in these three areas can be a source of strength for every other area of your life. Let's consider each of these in turn.

THE ROLE OF PRAYER

We have examined the importance of prayer in the life of the believer and seen that achieving a vital and growing prayer life is our high calling; yet it can be a tremendous struggle. The temper of the times, our own bad habits, and the enemy of our souls conspire to keep us from knowing the full and abundant life of prayer God intends for us. We have further seen that using the psalms as a basis for our prayers is not only very Biblical and in line with the tradition of great saints of the past, but it simply makes good sense. To approach the Lord in prayer, using words He Himself has provided, can help to ensure that our prayers will receive a more favorable hearing before the throne of grace. Now I want to suggest five specific ways that you can expect to know a more powerful and consistent life of prayer if you will commit yourself to entering into the discipline of praying the psalms.

A greater sense of the presence of God
First, once you have begun to feel at home in this discipline and have become comfortable using the various approaches to praying the psalms, you should begin to have more of a sense of being in the presence of God as you pray. How could it be otherwise? When our hearts and minds are engaged with God's Word, and when our mouths are offering His own words back to Him in the power of His Spirit, it stands to reason that we will become more acutely aware of actually being before His throne of grace, knowing the gaze of His countenance upon us, caught up in His power, and pouring out our hearts before Him with confidence and joy. As you follow God's prayer program you will begin to have

more of a sense of escaping your mundane existence and entering into the heavenly realm, where Christ stands to intercede for you at the Father's right hand.[2] Time will pass without your being aware of it, and you will experience a foretaste of eternity. As the words of the psalms expand your vision of God in all His beauty, holiness, and power, you will experience a greater joy and excitement in His presence and will find that your prayers will flow more readily as He leads you in His Word. You'll learn why great saints of the past referred to their time before the Lord as the "Sweet Hour of Prayer," and why they so often resorted to it with joy and anticipation.

I am convinced that one of the reasons that Christians do not pray any more than they do is that they have but little sense of being in the presence of God when they pray. Because of this, they do not feel as though their prayers have much power, and they seldom find them to be an exciting conversation with the Lord. But learning to pray the psalms can change this. Praying the psalms can bring us more readily and keep us more consistently in the very presence of God as we pray, helping us to focus on His glory and His will as we bring our praises, thanks, confessions, and requests before Him in the words that He has given us through His Spirit.

Greater consistency in prayer

Second, using God's prayer list can help to ensure that your prayers are more consistent, that is, that you will actually avail yourself of this discipline with greater frequency and regularity. Simply put, praying the psalms can help to ensure that you will pray more often. As with anything in life that we intend to master, it helps to have a plan and a schedule. Praying the psalms – especially if you are able to incorporate some of the hours of prayer into your daily life – will give you a means of turning to prayer more often, together with a plan for prayer that will help you to gain greater consistency and comprehensiveness in prayer over time.

As you grow in the sense of being in God's presence in prayer, the time you spend in prayer will increase out of a strong desire to be with the Lord, and not merely as some kind of duty to which you feel obligated or bound. You will be praying more, at more times during the day, and with greater satisfaction and assurance that your prayers are being effective before the Lord. This growing consistency in prayer will lend greater peace and satisfaction to your walk with the Lord overall, and you will have a greater sense of being in His presence throughout the day, with all your accounts clear and in order before Him (more on this in a bit). You will pray more because you want to, because you will be discovering just how sweet and powerful this time in the Lord's presence can be.

More comprehensiveness in prayer
Third, you will find that by praying the psalms you will cover more subject matter in your prayers than you ever have before. You will find more people

coming to mind in your prayers, more needs (even of people you do not know), more subjects for intercession, and more expressions of praise and thanksgiving than you have ever known. Plus you will find that many of those requests and people whom you formerly were only able to remember by recording them on a list are beginning to be imbedded in your heart, and that they come to mind readily and often during your prayers.

I find this to be especially true if I make a conscious effort to connect individual requests for prayer with particular psalms. Praying those psalms brings those requests to mind and helps me have greater confidence in bringing them to the Lord, since I am using words He Himself has provided. As I pray particular psalms I let my mind linger over them for a time, waiting to see what the Holy Spirit might bring to mind as a subject for specific prayer that I have not yet considered. Often, world situations, upcoming events, potential opportunities for ministry, the requests of others, or long-forgotten items of praise will come to my mind, and I will use the words of the psalm to direct my thoughts to the Lord as He may lead.

It is particularly satisfying to me to know that on a regular basis I am remembering to pray for things that only infrequently came into my mind before – such as the persecuted Church, the spiritual warfare in which I am daily engaged, the leaders of the Christian Church and the rulers of the nations, those who are in places of influence and power in our society, the hurting and defeated among the members of Christ's Body, and the lost among us. While I might have prayed for such matters only occasionally in the past, now they are part of my weekly discipline before the throne of grace, as the Lord leads me in His psalms to remember these and many, many more important subjects.

A greater sense of freedom in prayer
Fourth, praying the psalms will give you a greater sense of freedom in prayer. I can recall at times wondering whether or not the words I was using were appropriate; whether my attitude in prayer was what it should be; whether there were certain matters, heavy on my heart, that somehow were not quite appropriate for prayer; and whether I should talk to the Lord about certain things that I knew were not pleasing to Him about my life.

Praying the psalms has helped me to come to resolution concerning these and many other questions, and has freed me to pray more boldly and honestly before the throne of grace. The psalms allow me to be angry, fearful, hurt, depressed, and full of doubt, as well as exuberant and joyful. They let me express outrage at injustices done to the poor. The psalms guide me through confession of sin and help me to claim God's forgiveness and His renewing grace. They mark out a consistent pathway for my praise and thanksgiving. They allow me to move from shame to victory in the space of a single prayer; to express despair and confidence; to remember those who suffer and to share in the victories of those whom God is blessing.

I remember once reading about an experiment that was conducted with children in a school play yard. As long as that yard was unfenced, the children clustered near the middle of the playground, fearing to go too close to the road. Once a strong fence had been erected, however, they spread out to enjoy the whole playground. When the limits were clearly defined and a protective boundary put in place, the children were free to enjoy all the space provided for them. The psalms function something like that for me, providing a framework and a context, marking out the limits of the freedom I have in coming before the Lord in prayer.

Enrichment of all your prayers

Finally, praying the psalms as a daily discipline has enriched and enhanced all my other prayers as well. Invariably, whether I am praying over a meal, in a group, before an assembly or congregation, or in any other context, I find phrases or themes from the psalms creeping into my prayers. This is a great encouragement to me as I am praying and helps me to have a greater sense that these prayers, too, are pleasing to God and not merely self-serving or perfunctory routines. Sometimes it is necessary for me to spend long hours in my car. Rather than give all that time to listening to music or other diversion, I use a good portion of it for prayer, letting familiar psalms guide me as I pray and sing to the Lord.

What will your prayer life be like three years from now? Will you still be following the same routines, struggling with the same obstacles, and meeting with the same defeats in your prayers? Or will you find that your prayer life day by day is becoming more powerful and satisfying, that you have a greater sense of God's presence in prayer, and that your prayers are more pleasing to Him? Will your prayer life be growing more and more, so that you are daily making progress in realizing the apostle's injunction to pray without ceasing?[3] Praying the psalms as a daily discipline can help to make all these possible, and much more besides.

THE VISION OF UNSEEN THINGS

It is impossible to overestimate the importance of our being able to "see into" the realm of unseen things. Our practice of faith depends upon, as faith is the practice of unseen things, the outworking in our lives of convictions we hold about the spiritual realities which surround us.[4] The way to avoid being distracted and drawn off course by the temptations of this world is to train our minds to see into heavenly realities, where Christ is seated at the right hand of the Father, and our lives have been hidden with Him.[5] The Apostle Paul tells us that fixing our gaze on unseen realities can be a source of great strength in the midst of all kinds of trials.[6] There is no doubt that Scripture encourages, even commands us to develop the ability to see with the eye of faith into the unseen realities of the spiritual world. Praying the psalms can help us to achieve this objective in at least three ways.

Envisioning God's glory

The psalms go to great length to stimulate our imaginations concerning the majesty, splendor, and glory of God. He is likened to a devouring fire and a mighty wind rising over the whole earth.[7] We are invited to imagine His dwelling as spanning the seas and skies.[8] We see Him described in terms of majesty, splendor, light, clouds of darkness, and in many other ways. Why do the psalmists use these familiar images, exaggerated by hyperbole, as they lead us into the very throne room of God? Because this is how they want us to think of Him – as great, mighty, powerful, beautiful, exalted, brilliant like the sun, threatening like destructive forces, yet welcoming like a gracious Father. In our day a great deal of emphasis is being put on the fact of God as our Father – our Abba or "Daddy." We are encouraged to think of Him in warm and familiar terms, and to draw near in confidence that He welcomes and will receive us. All this is true; but it is only half the truth. God is a Being who should strike fear in our hearts. Throughout the Word of God, when His faithful people come into His presence, they experience both fear and wonder, a sense of dread as well as a sense of delight. This was their experience because their sense of God was full of the glorious images used in the psalms to portray Him to their thinking. Their imaginations were rich with images of God's glory, while their hearts were full of affections of gratitude, praise, and joy. Following God's prayer program can help us to regain this sense of who God is, and to see into the unseen realm where He rules in glory with Christ at His right hand.

The reign of Christ

Second, praying the psalms invites us to consider the reign of Jesus Christ in compelling terms. Psalm 2 portrays Him as exalted and receiving the nations as His inheritance. He rules them with a rod of iron and calls them to submit to His rule. Psalm 110 shows Him advancing His Kingdom on earth by enlisting His faithful people as servants of His rule. Psalm 45 depicts Him radiant in glory, receiving His bride as she approaches Him in the splendor with which He has adorned her. Various of the psalms portray the joy and power of His coming return in judgment.

There is a very familiar painting of Jesus standing outside a cottage, gently knocking on a door which has no handle. His head is slightly bent, as if listening to hear whether anyone inside will open the door and let Him come in. He is the picture of the perfect gentleman, calmly and quietly announcing His presence, humbly waiting to be granted permission to enter a private domain.

Try selling that image to the Apostle Paul. What Paul experienced on the road to Damascus was not the sweet Jesus of that painting, knocking gently on the door of Paul's heart, but the mighty Messiah he had been praying about all his adult life in the

Psalms, who came in a flash of brilliant light and laid hold on His chosen servant for the work of His Kingdom.

The Jesus of the psalms is a powerful Ruler. All the nations are in His hand, and all His people, together with all of creation, jump to the service of His Word and leap with joy at the prospect of His coming in judgment. When He does return He will scatter the bodies of those who failed to heed His knocking and gather His elect to Himself as a bride glorious in her beauty. All creation rejoices with unspeakable joy at the return of the Lord, who will make all things new, forever and ever, whose steadfast love endures forever and whose faithfulness is everlasting.

Praying the psalms can enhance our ability to see Jesus in this role, exalted at the Father's right hand, extending His rule over all the earth, and coming again in judgment. As we learn to see into this part of the unseen world more clearly and consistently, we will be more inclined to follow Him as obedient servants and to take up our callings as His witnesses, proclaiming that Christ is Lord and King and warning of judgment to come, even as we invite all to receive His love and forgiveness.

The vision of God's attending love

The psalms present God's love as steadfast and unfailing. He created us. He feeds and sustains us. His Spirit is ever attending to us. He watches over us from His throne. His angels come to our defense.

The thoughts He has toward us and the works He enters into on our behalf each day are more than we can even begin to count. We are always on His mind, and He is always at our side.

The psalms give new meaning to the promise of Hebrews 13:5 that our God will never fail us nor forsake us. They depict Him as gathering our food, preparing our work, seeking us out in our times of distress, coming to our defense against enemies, watching over us as we sleep, and searching the depths of our hearts and minds. The images by which the psalms invite us to pray with thanksgiving concerning all these matters are intended to fix in our minds the sense of God's presence with us throughout all the days of our lives. We begin to "see" the unseen world all around us, to experience the sudden intervention of angels, to be reminded of God's promises by the whispered word of His Spirit. The reality of what is going on around us all the time – the hubbub of an unseen realm that rules and directs and sustains all that is – will become more real to us as we allow our imaginations to traverse this territory through regular use of the psalms in prayer. Left to our own prayer lists and inclinations, our world can be pretty small – our own circle of interests, friends, and concerns. But by praying the psalms we are reminded of how vast the world is, and that the unseen world is a place of great energy where divine love is continuously directed toward us for our benefit and God's glory.

RELATIONSHIP WITH THE LORD

Finally, praying the psalms will help your prayer life to be more meaningful, more powerful, and more satisfying. It can also strengthen your walk with the Lord. I have found this to be true in five ways.

The sense of God's presence throughout the day
First, as you begin praying the psalms more consistently, and at more times during the day, you will have a greater sense of the Lord's presence in your life throughout the day, and not just when you are with Him in prayer. This is because of two things: (1) First, you will be praying more often during the day, taking time out for conversation with the Lord at regularly scheduled times. This cannot help but make you more conscious of His presence. (2) But second, you will find that ideas, themes, and phrases from the psalms begin to be more and more present to your subconscious mind, and will find their way into your thinking with greater frequency during the day.

This awareness of God's presence is a wonderful help for recognizing and resisting temptation, exercising good stewardship over time and resources, and facing every potentially threatening situation with peace and confidence. It will also help to keep you mindful of the fact that no area of your life is separate from the Lord and His interest in you. Nothing that you do is done apart from His presence; thus, everything must be done in a way that will bring honor and glory to Him. Your entire daily life

– even such mundane routines as taking out the trash or getting ready for the day – will become infused with a sense of God's presence and thus become areas of service for His glory. Praying the psalms will make you more aware of God's presence throughout your daily life, and will help to make you more conscious of wanting to serve Him in all you do.

God's glory in everyday experiences

Second, praying the psalms will give you more insight into the glory of God in the common experiences and everyday events of your life. While before you might have taken for granted the beauty of a stand of pine trees or the vast expanse of the sky, or have listened to a news report of some far-off tragedy in an indifferent manner, or read a poem or looked at a painting as little more than an object in itself, you will find that you cannot help but see in all these things expressions of the goodness and mercy of God; and you will be led to praise Him or to intercede for some need that you might otherwise have ignored.

Psalms 19 and 104 keep me mindful of God's sovereign care for His creation. I cannot help but think of them as I look out on the mountains near our home, or hear the wind rustling through the trees behind our home. Every rippling creek, craggy outcropping, or brightly colored bird reminds me of some psalm extolling the grace, strength, and beauty of the Lord. By praying Psalms 72 and 82 I am kept aware of the need for rulers to govern in just and caring ways. The psalms come to mind as I read a book or periodical or watch the evening news. Psalm 27 invites me to ask God to show His goodness to sufferers everywhere. With every new tragedy or desperate situation I find myself praying, "I would despair, O Lord, if I did not hope to see Your goodness in the land of the living",[9] as I pray for the needy or oppressed. Psalm 68 reminds me of God's many gifts to men and leads me to praise Him for all the ways I see His gifts expressed during the course of a day. As I pray through these and all the other psalms on a regular basis, their teaching becomes part of my outlook on life, leading me to see the glory of God – His mercy, compassion, and goodness – in almost everything around me. Thus I experience more and more each day the psalmist's joyful boast, "The earth is the LORD's and the fullness thereof..."[10] and I am filled with joy and hope throughout the day.

Strength for spiritual warfare

Third, you will find that praying the psalms gives you greater strength to prevail in the spiritual warfare. Every day spiritual forces of wickedness in high places are seeking to distract us from the Kingdom business to which God has called us and to defeat us in our desire to serve Him. Yet every day, and several times throughout the day, you will be in the presence of the Lord in prayer, seeking His strength and help against these terrible foes. I never cease to be amazed at how many of the psalms lend themselves to praying about spiritual warfare. Every one that mentions enemies can be profitably used to strengthen us against spiritual forces of wickedness that seek our undoing. Praying the psalms will bolster you in this fight, helping you to recognize temptation, giving you words in prayer for resisting the devil, and preserving you through temptation without falling into sin.

Every one of us struggles with besetting sins from time to time – anger, lust, indifference to suffering, fear, anxiety, stretching the truth, self-centeredness, lack of consideration for others, impatience, covetousness, doubt. But these besetting sins must not be allowed to become settled sins, that is, so settled in our lives that we have simply given up trying to overcome them. Praying the psalms can provide the perspective, rationale, and strength for dealing with every temptation that comes our way, and for helping us to break free from the besetting sins that plague us. We can actually grow in grace, knowing victory over temptation and sin in ever-increasing measure, and seeing Christ more perfectly formed in our lives, through submitting to the discipline of using God's prayer list. This will help us to be more effective not only in knowing His grace but in ministering it to others as well.

Knowing greater joy and peace

Fourth, praying the psalms can bring more of the joy and peace of the Christian life into your daily experience. In this world we have trouble, as our

Lord observed.[11] The pressures of our jobs, trials and challenges at home, financial difficulties, ruptured relationships, economic and social uncertainties, moral lapses, the treachery of a trusted friend, temptations of every sort – these are just a few of the trials and difficulties that we have to contend with every day. Focusing too intently on such matters can fill our lives with worry, fear, doubt, and anxiety. We need a larger frame of reference – a divine perspective – if we are going to know the overcoming power of our Lord Jesus Christ amid the pressures of everyday life.

Praying the psalms provides just such a perspective. As you labor in prayer through the psalms on a regular basis you will find that your vision of God is greatly enlarged, as we have seen. Your sense of His awesome power will be richly enhanced, and your confidence that He will strengthen and uphold you in the midst of every challenge or uncertainty will grow stronger every day. As a result, instead of falling into fear and depression in the face of your trials, you will be able to rejoice and be at peace, for you will know that the Lord who speaks to you in His psalms is with you to shield and guide you. You will find that your sense of expectancy is growing as you wait upon the Lord to see how He is going to provide for you in the midst of your trials. When your own words fail you at times of distress or disappointment, the words of the psalms will buoy and sustain you, lifting your eyes and spirit heavenward to wait upon the Lord Who cares for you and sovereignly rules in all your circumstances and situations. A peace that passes understanding and a joy inexpressible will begin more and more to be the context within which you engage your daily trials, as well as the power by which you overcome in the midst of them.

More of the full and abundant life

Finally, and as by now should be abundantly clear, praying through the psalms on a regular basis, and taking the time to do so more frequently during the day, will bring you a greater experience of the full and abundant life that Jesus promised to all who trust in Him. You will find that you have a greater dependence on those spiritual truths and realities that give ultimate meaning and purpose to our lives. Knowing the presence of God more intimately, you will be more consistently filled with joy in Him, and will be able to say with the psalmist, and truly mean it, "I have no good apart from you."[12] Your life will take on a more heavenly orientation; you will walk more consistently in hope and joy; prevail in the spiritual struggles that you encounter; have a better sense of being in tune with the presence of God in His creation; and be more involved in a deeply spiritual way with the needs and concerns of others. Your heart will be more full of thanksgiving and praise to God, and you will take joy in thinking about Him and all His lovingkindness, more than in any created thing that might formerly have been the key to your happiness. Your burden for the lost will increase. You will be more outspoken for your faith. You will grow in confidence that God's Kingdom will ultimately prevail against the wiles and schemes of all His enemies, and ours. You will desire to grow in grace and will work harder at crucifying the old person within you who still wants to hold on to sinful thoughts and ways. You will see everything in life more from the Lord's perspective and will find that the seas of your life are less and less disturbed by unexpected storms as you set your course on a closer walk with the Lord and trust in the psalter sail to carry you through.

These benefits – in prayer, in seeing through to the unseen realm, and in your relationship with the Lord – will neither come quickly nor suddenly. Rather, you will find them gradually falling into place as you press on in the discipline of praying the psalms. Three years from now your Christian life can be dramatically different – your prayers more powerful and meaningful and your walk with the Lord more abundant in every way – by your submitting to this discipline of praying the psalms, not in some perfunctory or Pharisaical manner, but with a full and expectant heart, a desire to grow in the Lord, and a commitment to using God's prayer program for the long haul.

But how will you be able to stay at this program in the face of the many temptations to forego it you can expect to encounter?

QUESTIONS FOR STUDY OR DISCUSSION

1. What goals have you set for your spiritual life for the coming year? In which areas of the spiritual life do you sense a need for greater growth? How can praying the psalms help you in these areas?

2. Consider the psalms you have begun to pray already. In what ways are you beginning to realize the promise of God's prayer program?

3. In which of the three areas outlined in this chapter would you like to see improvement in your life? How are trying to achieve that improvement at present? Can you see how praying the psalms could help in this?

4. What is keeping you from adopting God's prayer program? Talk with someone about these concerns.

5. Suppose you adopt God's prayer program. What obstacles can you anticipate in staying with the program?

---

[1] Eugene H. Peterson, *Answering God: The Psalms as Tools for Prayer* (New York: HarperCollins Publishers, 1991), pp. 3, 4.
[2] 1 John 2:1; Acts 7:56.
[3] 1 Thessalonians 5:17.
[4] Hebrews 11:1.
[5] Colossians 3:1-3.
[6] 2 Corinthians 4:17, 18.
[7] Psalm 50:3.
[8] Psalm 104:3.
[9] Psalm 27:13.
[10] Psalm 24:1.
[11] John 16:33.
[12] Psalm 16:2.

6.
STAYING WITH THE PROGRAM

CONCENTRATING ON THE SAIL
St. Brendan Foils the Devil

In bleakest blackness under a starless sky
St. Brendan stands a lonely watch. No light
or friendly landmark rises to meet his eye

or guide his course amid this darkest night,
the only sounds the slapping of the sea
against the curragh, and the flapping right

above him of the billowing sail. Yet he
is not afraid, content to let the breeze
from God determine what their course should be.

When suddenly, perched on the mast he sees
a horrifying sight: hell's foulest fiend
has lighted on their ship to tempt and tease

them, and to see if they might not be weaned
away from their obedience. "What brings you
unto us?" Brendan asked, as Satan preened

and pranced upon the mast, although he knew
the tempter's mission well. "These waters are
not safe on which you bring so small a crew

in this crude coracle on such a dark
and fearful night," replied the loathsome beast,
and then unveiled a terrifying, stark,

and dreadful vision of hell's fearful feast
to Brendan, such a vision that to see
it one would surely die. And though he ceased

not tempting till he thought the saint would be
undone, the gruesome fiend could not prevail
to make him change his course or quit the sea.

St Brendan met his every threat and wail
by concentrating on that billowing sail.

O God, you are my God; earnestly I seek you; my soul thirsts for you, as in a dry and weary land, where there is no water. So I have looked upon you in the sanctuary, beholding your power and glory.

- Psalm 63:1, 2

O God, my God, You, You alone are my God. I seek You in these times of prayer; I earnestly desire to meet You, to commune with You, to know Your presence and glory. My soul longs for You and greatly thirsts for You, but at times it is so hard to connect, so hard to feel Your presence and to know You are near. Help me to *persevere, to keep seeking You* and looking for You, that I might truly know Your power, and come into the presence of Your glory, and, in so doing, be transformed.

It is a gross understatement to say that you will be tempted, from time to time, to set aside the discipline of praying the psalms and to return to more familiar and less demanding approaches to prayer. You will be tempted *often* in this way.

There are a number of reasons for this. First, as I have suggested, praying the psalms is not something with which most of us are familiar. This discipline requires learning some new ways to pray, following unfamiliar protocols, making adaptations and adjustments according to your particular needs and circumstances, working hard to apply each psalm to your own life and those of the people for whom you are praying, and so forth. It will be frustrating at first. Any sense of progress may be slow in coming. It can seem so much easier just to work up a prayer list and let that be your guide each day.

Second, following God's prayer program will require more time and concentration in your prayers. The psalms will invite you to linger in prayer, and to seek more time for the Lord. You'll find yourself in a dialog with God in which, if you would truly benefit from the experience, you will need to give more earnest attention to His leadership in prayer. You may find it a challenge to your strength in prayer to work all the way through some of the psalms, particularly some of the longer ones, making the adaptations and applications that are necessary. You'll have to think harder than ever during your prayers, making interpretations and applications as you go and keeping in mind particular people and their needs as the Spirit leads.

Third, you may feel as though praying the psalms is not helping you to get at all the matters you think you need to in prayer. But this is just a matter of thinking more carefully about the way the psalms are guiding you, and being willing to take the time to reflect on the leading of the Spirit as He cues off any particular psalm to guide you in more specific prayer.

But the main reason you will be tempted to forsake this discipline was suggested in the superscription to the introduction to this book, and the little story of St Brendan's encounter with the enemy of our souls: The devil does not want you to pray, and he especially does not want you to pray the psalms; for he knows that *God's Word prayed by God's people before God's holy throne through the Name of God's Son and in the power of God's Spirit is a force too great for him to overcome.* His experience with the Lord Jesus in this regard was lesson enough.[1] If, therefore, he can discourage you from this discipline, it will be a major victory in his campaign against your maturing in the Lord and knowing more of the full and abundant life He has given you.

In this final chapter I want to suggest three ways of resisting the devil and dealing with the temptation to abandon God's prayer program as the foundation of your life of prayer. First, I will urge you not to "get under the pile" in using the psalms in your prayer. Second, I will encourage you to seek some accountability in the practice of this discipline. Finally, I will advise you to prepare yourself for the hard work of prayer and, thus, not to be surprised or alarmed when the temptation to abandon this discipline crops up before you, as it surely will.

DON'T GET UNDER THE PILE

Any time we submit to a regular schedule we run the risk of imposing a kind of legalism that can become oppressive. Anyone who has ever tried to get in shape or to lose weight can identify with this. We resolve to exercise for so many minutes, to run so many miles a week, to limit our intake of calories, or to lose so many pounds. Then we make schedules and promises to ourselves which can become difficult to keep, especially if we're not used to such a discipline. Before too long we find that we are skipping our exercises, fudging on our diet, and rationalizing our way around keeping the very disciplines we established in order to improve ourselves. A guilty conscience tells us to "get caught up," so we try to run further or eat even less or whatever, only to find ourselves continuing to fall behind in our regimen. At that point, we're not far from chucking the whole thing.

Praying the psalms presents a similar challenge. We set schedules, resolve to have a go at it, and get started with the best of intentions. Before too long, however, we find we have overslept one morning, or struggled with concentration during our prayers, or let something intrude on our schedule. A particular psalm absolutely stymies us, so we skip it, resolved to pick it up next time around. We feel somewhat restricted or artificial in our prayers. We don't immediately find this discipline as satisfying as we thought we would. We wonder whether this is such a good idea after all. And we're forever falling behind our schedule. Then we may start to feel a little guilty, so we determine to "get our act together" or get "caught up" on our praying at the next appointed time. That becomes a "rush-job" so that we can get back on schedule, and we know it, so we feel guilty or disappointed in ourselves all over again. Before long we will come to despise this discipline which holds such promise for our prayers. What we'd hoped would be smooth sailing in prayer has turned into the dark night of our souls, and we can't find any light to guide us. Then will come the temptation just to forget it and go back to something more familiar – even though that has never proven to bring the satisfaction and fulfillment we need in prayer.

Managing your time in prayer

The schedules that follow in the appendix are meant to suggest some ways of carrying out this discipline so that you can work your way through the entire psalter in a regular and timely manner. *But please note: You will not be able to keep any schedule perfectly*. We are not the lords of our time. God is the Lord of our time, and we are His stewards. He is free to do with our time whatever He pleases. Our responsibility, apart from doing our best to plan for the wise stewardship of our time,[2] is to make the most of every situation that He brings our way, even if it means a change in our plans is necessary some times.[3] You may oversleep some day, or have a meeting that runs through your planned time of prayer, or be in a situation where it is just not possible to pray a psalm before your meal. Or you may simply forget that you had scheduled time for prayer and go right on with your daily routine. None of these or any of a hundred other similar disruptions should cause you to set this discipline aside. Simply move on, looking ahead to your next appointed time of prayer, and not fussing or fuming over missing one session or having a session that seemed flat or lacking in power. You cannot recover lost time, and you cannot improve on time poorly used. The only time you have is the moment immediately at hand. Don't live in the past. Make the most of every opportunity the Lord gives you for meeting with Him in prayer, and work at making better use of your time in the days ahead.

Dealing with distractions

But there are some things you can do to make the best use of the time you have scheduled for prayer. One is learning to deal with distractions. At times during my own prayers I find it difficult to concentrate on the matter suggested by the psalms. So many things can come to mind or intrude on my prayers to distract me from my purpose. Just this morning, for instance, I was so distracted by a particular matter that I simply could not get it out of my mind. It was clouding every psalm I tried to pray, causing my prayers to be little more than empty exercises in useless utterance. So I stopped, spent some time in prayer over the particular matter that was distracting me so, and gave it to the Lord. Then I returned to my psalms. But the matter did not go away; and although it continued to linger in my mind, I had the assurance that God was taking care of this situation, and that helped me to concentrate rather more fully on the subject matter of the psalms before me.

Other potential distractions can be similarly dispatched: the phone rings while you are keeping an appointment for prayer – commit the caller's need to the Lord, and let the phone ring on. You suddenly have to break off your prayer to attend to an urgent situation – carry the essence of your prayer with you as you go, even, if possible, using the content of the psalm to prepare you for the matter to which you must now attend. You suddenly remember a deadline you simply have to meet – excuse yourself from prayer, praising the Lord for His longsuffering kindness, and promise to meet with Him again as soon as possible.

Distractions are simply that; you can learn to deal with each one in a manner appropriate to its unique challenge. But distractions need not be deal-breakers in praying the psalms. Let your prior commitment to mastering this discipline carry you through every distraction as you persevere in God's prayer program.

Resisting the devil

Do not let God's prayer program become in the devil's hands an instrument of self-tyranny. God's prayer program is meant to *help* our prayers, not put us under the pile. Whenever you begin to feel as though this is the case, that you are being overburdened, or becoming legalistic in your prayers just to keep up some program, slow down, cut back, but keep moving on to the next appointment for prayer and your next psalm. The tempter will look for every opportunity to discourage, distract, and defeat you. He does not want you following God's prayer program, praying the psalms. Remember that. The Scriptures tell us to resist the devil, and he will flee from us.[4] So when he comes to try to talk you out of this exciting but challenging discipline, recognize whose voice it is that is encouraging you to quit God's prayer program. Deal with each challenge as it comes. Submit to the Lord and press on, and you will find that you grow stronger each time you send the preening and prancing fiend away in disappointment and defeat.

BE ACCOUNTABLE

The Christian life works best when we are accountable to others for the commitments we make to the Lord. That's why the Lord Jesus sent His disciples out to preach two-by-two. It's the reason Paul consistently returned to Antioch to make report on his various missionary journeys. It's what motivated Paul to confront Peter in Antioch.[5] We need accountability if we are to grow, because, on our own, we are likely to cut corners and look for the easy way around the hard edges of discipleship.

When I first began to take up the challenge of praying the psalms I was meeting with my friend Steven Wright once a week for study and prayer. We talked often about the challenge of God's prayer program, and decided we wanted to know more about it. This led to our teaching a course together on using the psalms in worship, which meant we spent a great deal of time studying and planning and working out our individual assignments. Through it all Steven was a great encouragement to me in this discipline, and I'm convinced God used his enthusiasm for this project, and his example, to help me stay with God's prayer program in those early days.

These days my wife, Susie, is my accountability partner. We encourage one another in the practice of this discipline and share together what God is teaching us as we follow His program for our prayers. Her example and encouragement are a great stimulus to me in this endeavor.

Find an accountability partner

There are several ways that you can build more accountability into your prayers. First, let someone close to you know that you are undertaking to use the psalms in your prayers. Ask that person – a spouse or close friend, perhaps – to pray for you, as this will be a new challenge and a big struggle, at least for a while. You don't need to elaborate on the details of how often you plan to pray or which schedule you intend to follow. There is a danger of unconsciously flaunting your spirituality if you explain too much about the specifics of your plan. Just say that you are trying to let the psalms be your main prayer list, and ask for their support in prayer. Check in with your "prayer partner" from time to time, to report on your progress, seek prayer for any struggles, and express your appreciation for his or her loving support in this endeavor. Your partner's encouragement and prayers can play a huge role in helping you to make progress in staying with God's prayer program.

Attach requests for prayer to specific psalms
A second way to be accountable involves the requests for prayer that others bring to you. We all have the experience of people asking us to pray for this, that, and the other. There is nothing anyone can ask you to pray about that is not covered by one or another of the psalms. What I try to do when someone asks for special prayer is to attach that request to one of the psalms, either by a mental or written notation. Recently some friends in another state were going through a difficult time with one of their sons. They were filled with all kinds of questions – "Why is this happening?" "What are we going to do?" "What is the Lord trying to do in all this?" – and asked for our prayers. I immediately thought of Psalm 13 and resolved to pray for them as I came to that psalm in the normal course of my prayers. On many occasions I interact with pastors, who ask me to pray about one thing or another concerning their ministries. Since I pray for pastors and church leaders especially when I pray Psalms 82 and 87, it is easy enough for me to fit their requests into this part of my schedule. I find it tremendously satisfying to be able to say to someone, "I have been praying for your need, using the Lord's Word in the psalms," and to refer him or her to the particular psalm I have been praying. People have often found comfort in beginning to pray that psalm for themselves as well.

Pray the psalms with someone

A third way of being accountable in praying the psalms is to have someone you can pray with from time to time. This will be easier for some of us than for others; but if you have occasion to meet with a Christian friend from time to time, why not include a season of praying a psalm during your time together? Take a few moments to pray the psalm out loud, then use it as a guide for a time of prayer together. You can do the same in church meetings, Bible study groups, or at home with your family. The joy and satisfaction that come from doing this with others will reinforce your commitment to continue praying the psalms as a daily discipline.

Being accountable in prayer will help you to get started in the discipline of praying the psalms and enable you to get over some of the rough spots you can expect to encounter. It will also help you in connecting the psalms with particular needs and requests and give you the delight of praying with another as the Lord leads in His Word. Such accountability will help you to get through many of the dark nights of temptation that will find you wondering about whether or not this discipline is for you.

WORK HARD AT PRAYER

The monks of the Middle Ages used to call prayer "the labor of God." Prayer is hard work. We should not expect it to be like sleeping, where all we have to do is lie still until we drift off; or eating, where every bite of food is a delight and we don't stop until we're full. Prayer is hard work, and, like any hard work, it means getting "sore muscles" until we have mastered the disciplines that go into it. Staying with God's prayer program can be particularly daunting, for all the reasons we have outlined above. It means encountering new problems and challenges that we have to work through or around. It means adjusting, adapting, and accommodating to new circumstances and situations; mastering new skills and techniques; putting up with intrusions and disruptions without losing sight of the goal. It means having to do battle with the devil in ways we never have before.

But just because our *work* is hard, and each day at the office or school is filled with plenty of challenges, we don't walk away from it and go out for a round of golf – not every day anyway. We stay on task, persevering through every obstacle because we know the job needs to get done and we understand and accept our responsibilities. If we don't work, we don't eat; so, no matter how difficult or discouraging it can be, we stay at our work, and don't give up.

The fight of your life!

We need to have the same attitude toward prayer, especially toward using God's prayer program. Make up your mind from the beginning that you are entering into the fight of your life. Start small, but with a determination to stay at it for the long haul. Take your time and gradually work up to a full schedule of praying the psalms on a regular basis. Expect to encounter discouragement and distractions. But let every temptation to give up be a summons to recall the many benefits that can come from staying the course with this discipline. Be accountable for your prayers. Expect to be tested, tried, and wearied as a result. You won't be disappointed. The only lasting disappointment that can come from God's prayer program is in failing to gain all that God has planned for us in it, all the promise of this program that we examined in the last chapter. Like Jacob wrestling with the angel, stay with the program. Persist, persevere, and keep your eye focused on God, believing that His Spirit will fill the sails of your psalm-filled prayers and bring you through every difficulty and trial to smoother sailing and greater blessing.

Send the devil packing!

An old spiritual says, "The devil, he has a slippery shoe, and if you don't watch out, he'll slip it on you." This will never be truer than when you have to struggle with him over this matter of using God's prayer program. Your "prayer feet" will feel cramped and tired with this discipline at times, and he'll hold out the smooth slippers of some other approach or even no approach at all. But God's Word is alive and powerful. God's Spirit, Who gave the words of the psalms, is able to intercede for us with these words He has given. The devil will try to block your use of the psalms in prayer by every means at his disposal, because he does not want to have to deal with the kind of power that praying the psalms arrays against him. Better if he can keep you from the discipline of prayer – and of praying the psalms in particular – as often as he can.

Like Brendan on that dark night of temptation, listen for the billowing of the sail as the Spirit of God calls you to the psalms as His program of prayer for you. Don't listen to the voice that says you should not be doing this, you don't know what you're doing, this isn't right for you, and all the rest. Remember the example of the saints of Scripture and of Church history. Recall the promises of following God's prayer program. Resolve to face up to the challenge in the power of God's strength, and send the devil packing as you stay the course with God's prayer program and continue to trust Him to make this discipline the blessing and source of power it has been for countless saints throughout the ages.

I can think of no better way of bringing this study to a close than by recommending these words by my friend, Steven Wright:[6]

Borrowed Words

It is a justifiable theft
This praying of borrowed words.
My own words gave out years ago
Like the wind when a ship hits the doldrums.
I drifted
Prayerless
Until I learned how to borrow words.

Now the pleas of Heman and Solomon
The plaints of Asaph and David

163

Propel me on
As they leap from my lips
Heavenward,
Carried by Christ.

They were his words at first,
Borrowed by psalmists
And borrowed back when
Hanging on the cross he cried,
My God, My God, why hast Thou forsaken me?
Surely, my God,
Thou wilt not forsake me
If I borrow Thy words
And offer them back to Thee.

QUESTIONS FOR STUDY OR DISCUSSION

1. What concerns, reluctances, or questions do you yet have about taking up God's program of prayer? Review chapters 1-5 to see if they can help.

2. Is it reasonable to expect that using the psalms as the basis for our prayers should be a difficult discipline to master? Why? How will you prepare to overcome the difficulties you can expect to encounter?

3. Can you think of someone who might be willing to hold you accountable for praying the psalms? Or to join you in praying them some times? Talk to that person concerning the matter.

4. Over the next couple of weeks, read the Book of Psalms through as part of your daily Bible reading. Make note of any psalms that seem to speak to you in a special way. Select one or two of them and begin praying them. Set a new time to pray the psalms each day.

5. Did you reach the goals you set for this study? What goals would you like to set for going on with praying the psalms?

---

[1] Matthew 4:1-11.
[2] Psalm 90:12.
[3] Ephesians 5:15-17; Acts 16:4-7.
[4] James 4:7.
[5] Galatians 2:11-14.
[6] This poem appeared in *Christianity and the Arts*, Spring, 2000, p. 11, and is used by permission of the author.

Appendix 1: Schedules

In this appendix I have included three schedules for praying through the psalms on a regular basis. The first is for praying the psalms over the period of a month. The second takes you through the psalms in a week. The last one is a suggested schedule for praying through the psalms on a single day devoted to solitude with the Lord.

The first schedule recommends three different periods of prayer during the day – morning devotions, mid-day, and evening. The morning period consists (in most cases) of three periods of prayer, an initial prayer of praise and thanksgiving, a portion of Psalm 119 or another psalm related to hearing God in His Word, which is to be used prior to Bible reading or study, then a psalm of intercession to guide your morning prayers. The mid-day period consists of various psalms of intercession, supplication, or complaint. The evening psalm is generally one of praise or resting in the Lord.

The second schedule recommends seven periods of prayer, as indicated on the schedule (although the first two are generally kept together in practice). In this schedule the Hebrew words indicated at the beginning of the devotions period of prayer represent sections of Psalm 119 and are usually marked as such in English Bibles. In this schedule an effort has been made to group psalms related to the passion of our Lord at the times of the week when the events suggested would actually have taken place.

The final schedule suggests two approaches to praying through the psalms on a single day devoted entirely to prayer.

Just a reminder not to let yourself become discouraged in taking up one of these schedules for praying through the entire psalter, or in creating one of your own. Perhaps you will begin with one part of the schedule – say, one of the set times each day – for a couple of weeks, until that has become fairly regular. Then you can add another of the times, and continue doing so until, over a period of weeks or months, you have incorporated the entire schedule into your daily prayer program. Let the schedule guide you, but don't allow it to enslave you, so that you end up despising this discipline rather than finding great delight and satisfaction in it. Begin small, and grow your involvement as the Lord enables you do so.

For a more traditional arrangement of the psalms for prayer, see Ronald Quillo, *The Psalms: Prayers of Many Moods* (New York: Paulist Press, 1999), pp. 11 ff.

PRAYING THE PSALMS THROUGH IN A MONTH

	Sun	Mon	Tue	Wed	Thu	Fri	Sat
Wk. 1	16, 119:1-8, 44, 122, 80, 4	9, 59, 119:9-16, 27, 46, 63	8, 119:17-24, 90, 116, 138	96, 119:25-32, 7, 71, 21, 110	108, 119:33-40, 97, 107, 117, 109	113, 119:41-48, 111, 22, 145	147, 119:49-56, 56, 70, 133, 1
Wk. 2	121, 119:57-64, 10, 45, 123, 3	146, 119:65-72, 115, 112, 149	148, 119:73-80, 88, 131, 91	92, 119:81-88, 132, 58, 130, 134	47, 119:89-96, 57, 61, 75	48. 119:97-104, 73, 69, 86	136, 119:105-112, 129, 137, 43, 28

	Sun	Mon	Tue	Wed	Thu	Fri	Sat
Wk. 3	30, 119:113-120, 50, 11, 14	66, 119:121-128, 17, 64, 20, 114	144, 119:129-136, 5, 28, 13, 65, 150	106, 119:137-144, 83, 124, 15, 24	2, 119:145-152, 25, 120, 6	34, 119:153-160, 94, 23, 67, 62	76, 119:161-168, 72, 26, 87
Wk. 4	105, 119:169-176, 49, 84, 127, 141	139, 19, 60, 81, 126, 99	104, 12, 37, 42, 31	103, 33, 36, 38, 39, 53	40, 29, 35, 74, 41, 52, 55	51, 89, 98, 78, 82, 93, 100	85, 32, 68, 77, 108
Wk. 5	101, 143, 118, 79, 54, 125	135, 95, 140, 102, 142					

PRAYING THE PSALMS THROUGH IN A WEEK

	Sun	Mon	Tue	Wed	Thu	Fri	Sat
Rising:	3, 9, 16, 112, 139	8, 45, 48, 112, 147	5, 18, 66, 99	15, 49, 93, 105	28, 68, 100, 104	29, 33, 71, 136	30, 47, 135, 142
Devotions:	Aleph-Gimel 51, 73, 77, 95	Daleth-Vav 6, 19, 53, 72	Zayin-Tet 12, 67, 88, 114	Yod, Lamed 7, 26, 37, 101	Mem-Samek 36, 39, 94, 148	Ayin-Tsadeh 32, 102, 127, 141	Ooph-Tau 38, 57, 61, 86
Mid-am:	2, 50, 78, 122	10, 43, 81, 144	27, 79, 83, 90	70, 80, 82, 97	13, 87, 106, 140	17, 56, 59, 62	40, 64, 98, 132
Noon:	46, 92	21, 91	23, 117	121, 131	20, 24	85	25
Mid-p.m.	14, 74, 84, 118	58, 76, 96, 120	44, 52, 89, 129	35, 54, 60, 130	42, 116, 124	22, 31, 34, 69	65, 103, 137
Evening:	1	108	75, 115	11, 133	125	107	128, 134
Retiring:	63, 138	4, 110	113, 145	11, 133	41, 55, 109	123, 126	149, 150

PRAYING THROUGH THE PSALMS IN A DAY DEVOTED TO PRAYER

Now this will obviously be a most challenging experience. However, taking a day away for prayer is not an uncommon practice. Many Christians do so from time to time, just as did the Lord Jesus Christ.

The schedules on the preceding pages can be adjusted or adapted as you see fit to allow you to use any or all of the psalms as part of a day devoted to the Lord in prayer. Such a practice can be daunting, to be sure, but it can also yield spiritual refreshment and renewal of a very high order.

For this activity, either of the preceding schedules can be followed. Simply divide your day into either three or seven periods of prayer, then, using the schedule for monthly praying (if you have chosen three periods) or for weekly praying (if you have chosen seven), fill your periods of prayer accordingly. You'll use the same amount of time either way – the whole day; you'll simply be following a different schedule for your prayers. If you are using the monthly schedule, you will need to pray all the first hour psalms (for the whole month) in your first period, the second hour psalms in your second period, and the third hour psalms in your third period. If you follow the weekly schedule, pray the Rising psalms (for the whole week) during your first period, and so on to completion.

You can make a day devoted to prayer a richer experience by singing some of the psalms in your schedule. Appendix 2 provides numerous examples of psalms set to familiar hymns for singing. Check the hymnal used in your church. It will also have quite a few hymns which are comprised of or based on psalms. Integrate these into your day of prayer, and you'll find that it can be a much richer experience over all.

Appendix 2: Psalms for Singing

Singing the psalms can add a most rewarding dimension to God's prayer program. Believers throughout the centuries have found in singing the psalms a rich supplement to their prayers, providing them with a source of joy, hope, and renewed faith at all times of the day and night. The psalms in this appendix are meant to represent the kinds of moods and themes that one encounters throughout the psalms. I recommend singing them aloud until they are learned by heart and are available for singing whenever the Spirit of God leads.

Psalms of Praise

Psalm 8

Tune: Aurelia – "The Church's One Foundation"
O Savior, how majestic, Your name in all the earth!
The heav'ns display Your glory and tell Your wondrous worth!
From babes and nursing infants, Lord, let Your strength increase
Till all Your foes surrender, and all their boastings cease.

When I regard Your heavens, Your handiwork above,
Ordained by Your good pleasure, according to Your love,
Then what am I, O Savior, that You take thought of me?
Or I should know Your favor and thus delivered be?

Yet we in Your own image with glory have been crowned,
To worship and to serve You throughout creation 'round.
These works that sing Your glory in our poor hands are placed,
That we may rule before You to magnify Your grace.

Let every beast and creature in sky or sea or field
In our hands bring Your glory as we Your favor wield!
Let all things sing Your praises, let all declare Your worth:
O Savior, how majestic Your name in all the earth!

PSALM 19

Tune: St Christopher – "Beneath the Cross of Jesus"

The heav'ns declare God's glory, the skies His work proclaim!
From day to day and night by night they shout His glorious name!
No speech, no words, no voice is heard, yet all across the earth
The lines of His all-present Word make known His holy worth!

Behold, the sun arises, a bridegroom strong and bright,
Rejoicing as he runs his course from morning unto night.
From east to west across the skies his circuit he completes,
And none can hide his sinful eyes or shelter from his heat.

The Law of God is perfect, His testimony sure;
The simple man God's wisdom learns, the soul receives its cure.
God's Word is right, and His command is pure, and truth imparts;
He makes our eyes to understand, with joy He fills our hearts.

The fear of God is cleansing, forever shall it last.
His judgments all are true and just, by righteousness held fast.
O seek them more than gold most fine, than honey find them sweet;
Be warned by every word and line, be blessed with joy complete.

Who, Lord, can know his errors? O keep sin far from me!
Let evil rule not in my soul that I may blameless be.
O let my thoughts, let all my words, before Your glorious sight,
Be pleasing to You, gracious Lord, acceptable and right!

PSALM 138

Tune: Regent Square – "Angels From the Realms of Glory"

I will give You thanks and praises, God of gods, with all my heart!
I will bow before Your temple, grateful praise to You impart!
For Your name and for Your glory, You have magnified Your Word.

All earth's kings will shout Your story when Your Word of truth they hear.
Of Your ways and of Your glory gladly let them shout and cheer!
For the proud shall not approach You, yet You hold the lowly dear.

On the day we call You hear and make us bold within our soul.
Though we in a place of fear stand, You revive and make us whole.
For Your hand will gently shield us, and our fearsome foes control.

Your Right Hand will save and keep us; all we need You will supply.
For Your love is everlasting, reaching from above the sky.
You will not forsake or leave us; You will save us when we cry!

Psalms of Pleading for Help

PSALM 10

Tune: Aberystwyth – "Jesus, Lover of My Soul"

Why stand off, O Lord, afar? Why in times of trouble hide?
Wicked men in foolish pride seek Your precious flocks to harm.
Many plots do they devise; catch them in their wicked schemes!
Greed and lust fill all their dreams, while they curse You, God most wise.

Wicked men in boastful pride seek not, Lord, Your glorious face.
To their shame and great disgrace, they Your existence have denied.
Still they prosper every day; from their sight on high concealed
Your great wrath shall be revealed on their every word and way.

Boastfully they scorn their foes: "We shall not be moved!" they cry.
With their tongues they curse and lie, sure they will never suffer woes.
See they stalk the poor and meek, lurking like a stealthy lion.
They would full devour Zion, crust the afflicted and the weak.

"Where, O where is God?" they say; "He has hidden out of sight!"
Rise up, Lord, in all Your might! Rescue all who You obey.
Wicked men Your judgment scorn; You observe their sinful ways.
Be our refuge, be our stay! Break the oppressor's evil arm.

Evermore, Lord, You will reign! Nations perish from Your land.
You will with Your people stand: Hear our cries of woe and pain!
Strengthen now our hearts, O Lord; vindicate Your people dear.
Drive away our ever fear; help and preserve us by Your Word.

PSALM 57

Tune: Faben – "Praise the Lord, Ye Heavens Adore Him"

Lord, be gracious, gracious to me, for my soul retreats in You.
In Your shadow keep me safely till the storms of life are through.
I will cry to You, the Most High; You do all things well for me.
You will save me when I thus cry, routing all who threaten me.

Send Your truth and lovingkindness; raging lions seek my soul.
Threats and sland'rous words without rest they against me fiercely roll.
Be exalted o'er the heavens, let Your glory fill the earth!
To Your name all praise be given; let all men proclaim Your worth!

Nets and pits they set before me; overwhelmed, my soul bows down.
Let them all in their own works be thrown and scattered on the ground.
Let my heart no more be shaken; I will sing Your praises, Lord!
Harp and glory, now awaken to extol God's faithful Word.

Praise and thanks among the nations I will sing with all my might,
For Your truth and love are stationed far above the highest height!
Be exalted o'er the heavens, let Your glory fill the earth!
To Your name all praise be given; let all men proclaim Your worth!

PSALM 70

Tune: Slane – "Be Thou My Vision"

O God, to rescue me do not delay!
Let those who seek me be turned back, I pray.
Bring them to shame who would bring me to strife.
Humble, dishonor those who seek for my life.

Let them be turned back because of their shame
Who would bring trouble and harm to my name;
Let all who seek You be glad and rejoice.
Let them salvation proclaim with their voice!

Let all who love You Your name magnify!
Hear the afflicted and needy who cry:
"Hasten to help us, O Savior, we pray!
God, our Deliverer, O do not delay!"

Psalms of Confession

PSALM 6

Tune: Lancashire – "Lead On, O King Eternal"

O Lord, do not rebuke me, nor chasten me in wrath;
Let graciousness and love be companions on my path.
I long to be restored, Lord, repentance is my song;
Receive my fainting word, Lord: How long, O Lord, how long?

My broken spirit rescue; O Lord, restore my soul!
No hope have I unless You return and make me whole.
O Lord, let lovingkindness prevail or I shall die!
In death who shall Your name bless, who shall Your praises cry?

I weep, and weary sighing, by night pour forth my tears.
I cease not from my crying and tremble in my fears.
My foes array before You; they bring my soul to grief.
My wasting eyes implore You: Lord, bring my soul relief!

Let all who sin delight depart from me in haste.
My prayers have entered right in before my Savior's face.
My foes turn back in anguish; they are no longer there!
My enemies are vanquished, for God has heard my prayer!

PSALM 32

Tune: Hendon – "Take My Life, and Let It Be"
Blessed are they whose sins the Lord has forgiven by His Word.
Pure their spirits are within; them He charges with no sin,
Them He charges with no sin!

When in silence I remained, groaning in my sinful pain,
Lord, Your hand upon me lay; all my strength You drained away;
All my strength You drained away.

I confessed my sin to You; You forgave me, ever true!
Let confession's pleading sound reach You while You may be found,
Reach You while You may be found.

When flood waters threaten me, You my hiding place will be.
O'er them I will rise above, buoyed by Your redeeming love,
Buoyed by Your redeeming love.

Teach me, Lord, how I should live; sound instruction ever give.
Let me never stubborn be; let Your eye watch over me;
Let Your eye watch over me.

Though the wicked wail and weep, they rejoice whose souls You keep!
Trusting, they exult with praise, joyfully singing all their days,
Joyfully singing all their days!

PSALM 38

Tune: Leoni – "The God of Abraham Praise"

O Lord rebuke me not, nor chasten me in wrath!
Your arrows pierce my sinful heart and fill my path.
Your heavy hand weighs down; my flesh and bones grow weak.
My sins oppress, confuse, confound – I cannot speak!

My sinful wounds grow foul, and fester painfully.
I bend and groan within my soul most mournfully!
Sin fills my every part; conviction stings my breast.
Lord, ease my numbed and burning heart and grant me rest!

You know all my desire; my sighs You know full well.
My strength fails and light's holy fire my eyes dispel.
My friends and loved ones fail; the wicked do me wrong.
My life they seek, my soul assail, the whole day long.

Their threats I will not heed, nor speak to their reproof.
To hear or speak I have no need; I claim Your truth!
Lord, hear my fervent prayer! Let not my foes rejoice!
Redeem me from their traps and snares – Lord, hear my voice!

My sins I now confess; my anxious soul relieve!
Though foes are strong, Lord heal and bless all who believe!
Forsake me now, O Lord! Repay my foes with wrath.
Stand by me with Your saving Word and guard and my path.

Psalms for the Pursuit of Righteousness

PSALM 1

Tune: St Thomas – "I Love Thy Kingdom, Lord"

How blessed are they that shun sin's vain and sinful and wicked ways.
For them has Christ salvation won; He loves them all their days!

God's Word is their delight; they prosper in its truth.
In it they dwell both day and night and flourish and bear fruit.

Firm planted on the banks of God's great stream of grace,
They raise unending praise and thanks to His great glorious face.

The wicked are not so, but, driven by the winds,
They fall and perish, weighed with woe, when once God's wrath begins.

In Jesus' righteousness, though sinners fail and fall,
His flock He will preserve and bless, who on His favor call.

PSALM 36

Tune: Landus – "My Faith Has Found a Resting Place"
Transgression speaks within the heart of him who fears not God.
He swells with pride to flaunt his sin and boasts in wicked words.
He ceases to be good or wise; he plots a wicked way.
His pathway is unrighteousness and evil all the day.

Your lovingkindness, Lord, is great, it reaches heav'n above.
Your faithfulness climbs to the skies and keeps us in Your love.
Your righteousness like mountains high, Your judgment like the deep
Preserve Your creatures great and small, and in Your mercy keep.

How precious is Your grace, O Lord; we shelter 'neath Your wings.
We drink refreshment to the full from Your abundant springs.
You give us freely of Your grace, we drink it with delight.
Life's fountain is with You, O Lord; in Your light we see light.

O let Your grace continue, Lord, to those who know You well.
Grant righteousness to all who trust and Your salvation tell.
Keep wickedness and pride away; Lord, keep us in Your grace!
For sinners fall before Your wrath, rejected from Your face.

PSALM 84

Holy Manna – "Brethren, We Have Met to Worship"
Lord of Hosts, how sweet Your dwelling! How my soul longs for Your courts!
Let my soul with joy keep telling of Your grace forevermore.
Like a bird upon the altar, let my life to Your belong.
Blessed are they who never falter as they praise Your grace with song.

Blessed are they whose strength is founded in Your strength, O Lord above.
All whose hearts are in You grounded journey in Your strength and love.
Though they weep with tears of sadness, grace shall all their way sustain.
In Your presence, filled with gladness, they shall conquer all their pain.

Lord of Host, my prayer receiving, hear me, help me by Your grace!
In Your courts I stand believing; turn to me Your glorious face!
Lord, our Sun, our Shield, our Glory, no good thing will You deny
To those who proclaim Your story and who on Your grace rely!

Psalms of Imprecation and Intercession

PSALM 2

Tune: Agincourt – "O Love, How Deep, How Broad, How High"

Why do the nations vainly rage, conspiring together from age to age?
Earth's kings and all their counselors stand against the Lord and His Right Hand:

"Now let us cast His yoke below, His Kingdom authority overthrow!
Throw off His Law, reject His Word, no more be governed by this Lord!"

The Lord in heaven laughs in wrath at all who embark on this cursed path.
His angry Word to them is plain: "Yet shall My King in Zion reign!"

Proclaim the message far and wide that God has exalted the Crucified!
From heav'n He sent His only Son, who has for us salvation won.

To Christ the Lord be given all who humbly embrace Him and on Him call.
Be wise, be warned: His judgment comes to break the prideful, sinful ones.

Rejoice with fear in Jesus' grace, and worship before His exalted face!
Beware His anger and judgment grim: How blessed are all who rest in Him.

PSALM 14

Tune: St. Anne – "Our God, Our Help in Ages Past"

The fool within his heart proclaims, "There is no God at all!"
His deeds are wicked, filled with shame, who on God will not call.

No good in such as these is found; corruption fills their breast.
God from His heav'ly throne looks down, their hearts and ways to test.

None understands, none seeks the Lord; they all have turned aside.
Deception leads them from God's Word who have His grace denied.

The workers of iniquity consume God's sheep like bread.
They trust not in the Lord, and He shall fill their hearts with dread.

For Jesus with the righteous stands, though they be put to shame.
He holds them safely in His hands who shelter in His name.

Restore Your Church, let Zion sing; our captive hearts release,
That we may Your salvation bring, rejoicing and in peace!

PSALM 72

Tune: Martyrdom – "Alas, and Did My Savior Bleed?"
O give the king Your judgment, Lord, and righteousness his son;
And let him judge by Your good word the need of everyone.

Let now the mountains ring with peace, the hills in righteousness;
Let justice rise, oppression cease, and all the needy bless.

Let nations fear You while the sun and moon endure on high.
Refresh, renew us, every one, like sweet rain falling from the sky.

Let righteousness abundant be where Jesus' reign endures!
Let peace increase from sea to sea till moonlight shall be no more.

The Lord the needy rescues when he cries to Him for grace;
All they who suffer violence find mercy in His face.

Let Christ be praised and all the gold of Sheba be His right;
Let blessings to His name be told and prayers made both day and night.

And let the earth abound with grain, let fields His fame proclaim;
And may our King forever reign and nations bless His name.

Now bless the God of Israel who wondrous works performs,
And bless His name, His glory tell, both now and forevermore!

Appendix 3:
A Topical Index of Psalms

Here is an index of the psalms by topic. You can use this when you want to spend time in prayer for a particular subject or need. These are not the only categories one might imagine for indexing the psalms, nor are they absolute in any sense. Several psalms could be put in more than one category, although I have only listed each psalm once. This listing, however, should be a helpful tool for categorical praying using the psalms.

For Confession of Sin
6, 7, 32, 38, 39, 41, 51, 77, 78, 86, 130

For Evangelism and Mission
47, 48, 49, 57, 60, 67, 107, 108, 110

For Imprecation and Intercession
2, 10, 11, 14, 17, 20, 35, 52, 53, 55, 58, 70, 71, 75, 83, 94, 109, 114, 115, 129, 137

For Pleading for Help
3, 4, 12, 13, 30, 31, 42, 43, 54, 56, 59, 61, 62, 64, 79, 88, 91, 120, 121, 123, 134

For Praise and Thanksgiving
8, 9, 16, 18, 19, 21, 22, 29, 33, 34, 45, 46, 65, 66, 68, 69, 76, 92, 93, 95, 96, 97, 98, 99, 100, 103, 104, 105, 111, 112, 113, 116, 117, 118, 135, 136, 138, 144, 145, 146, 147, 148, 149, 150

For Pursuing Righteousness
1, 5, 15, 23, 24, 25, 26, 27, 28, 36, 37, 40, 50, 63, 84, 90, 101, 119, 128, 130, 139

For Revival and Renewal
44, 74, 80, 81, 85, 89, 102, 106, 122, 126

For Rulers and Leaders
72, 82, 87, 127, 131, 133

For Times of Temptation and Trial
73, 124, 125, 140, 141, 142, 143

Other Books of Interest from
Christian Focus Publications

T. M. MOORE

Think of T.M. Moore's work as high-octane fuel... I pray it will ignite churches with longing for a true visitation of God in our time.
John Armstrong

PREPARING YOUR
CHURCH FOR
REVIVAL

Preparing your Church for Revival

T.M. Moore

We all long for revival, but we tend to pray for it to come without being completely sure what precisely revival is. This book will be a revitalising aid to those of us who desire revived spiritual life for our churches. T.M. Moore offer practical advice on steps, each with secure scriptural foundations, that we can take to prepare our churches for the sovereign work that is revival. This book is clear that there is no conflict between revival being a work of God and the continued and urgent need for God's people to earnestly pray for its appearance.

With practical guides to prayer for revival T.M. Moore realises the need for balance and succeeds in providing a book that will help us to refocus on revival, and will prepare our souls and our churches for the mighty work of a Sovereign and loving God.

'Think of T. M. Moore's work as high-octane fuel, written by a man who loves the church of Jesus Christ and longs to see her full of his glory once again. I pray his 'fuel' will ignite churches with longing for a true visitation of God in our time.'

John Armstrong

ISBN 1-85792-698-6

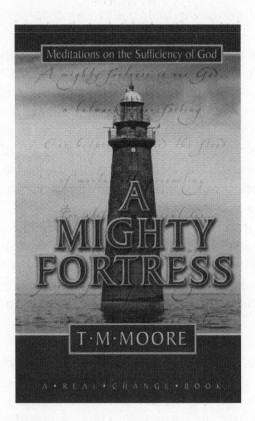

Meditations on the Sufficiency of God

A MIGHTY FORTRESS

T·M·MOORE

A · REAL · CHANGE · BOOK

A Mighty Fortress

Meditations on the Sufficiency of God

T M Moore

A Real Change book

God writes a lyric through our life. Through the means of praise and worship we can express our spiritual yearnings in ways that we would find difficult in everyday words or conversation.

Yet lyrics to hymns and songs become dry on our tongues. What once seemed to express our joy with incandescence, now glows feebly. We move on to new songs, only for the pattern to repeat itself. Nothing seems to last.

The problem is not the song, the problem is OUR song.

Using the verses from the great hymn 'A Mighty Fortress is our God', written from Martin Luther's meditations on psalm 46, T. M. Moore helps us recapture our song, written by God's hand in our life.

Rekindle the flames of your spiritual life and have a firmer footing to face the future.

At trying times Luther would turn to his closest friend and say 'Come Philip*, let us sing the 46th.' May your life also be turned into a more joyful song by staying in harmony with the God of all Creation.

* Philip Melancthon

ISBN 1-85792-868-7

Finding the Life You're Longing for from Psalm 23

SONG OF A
SATISFIED
SOUL

JOHN A. KITCHEN

'The ideal book to share with those needing encouragement.'
Warren W. Wiersbe

A · REAL · CHANGE · BOOK

Song of a Satisfied Soul

Finding the Life You're Longing for from Psalm 23

John A. Kitchen

A Real Change book

'The ideal book to share with those needing encouragement.'

Warren W. Wiersbe

'...beautifully sketches for us the one true source of true contentment. It will make the reader see a familiar passage of scripture from a fresh outlook. A must for anyone searching for true satisfaction and renewal in a world full of need.'

Rajendra Pillai
Reaching the World in Our Own Backyard

'Shot through with vivid illustrations and stories, "The Song of a Satisfied Soul" is going to end up at bedsides, in hip pockets, and handbags, and on preachers' desks.'

Richard Bewes

In the 23rd Psalm God lifts before us the song of the satisfied soul. It's the promise of a life better than you've dreamt possible. God offers us in the intimacy of a personal relationship with Himself. God Himself is our song, the singer, and the substance of the Song of the Satisfied Soul.

John A. Kitchen is a Pastor and author from Ohio
ISBN 1-85792-942-X

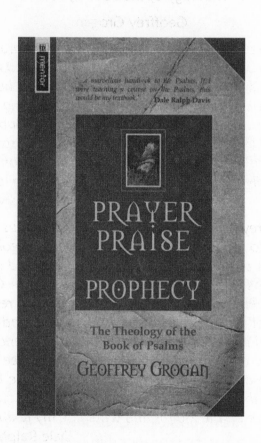

Prayer, Praise and Prophecy

A Theology of the Book of Psalms

Geoffrey Grogan

'Geoffrey Grogan's name is sufficient to guarantee a quality work, a high doctrine of Scripture and impeccable scholarship. The latter is carried lightly, but with sharp discernment of what is biblically sound, what is practically useful, and what outruns available evidence. If Grogan writes with one eye on the specialist 'state of play', the other eye is firmly fixed on being biblically illuminating to any and every Bible lover.'

Alec Motyer

'Geoffrey Grogan has given us a marvellous handbook to the Psalms. He does not tack on theological themes at the end but places them front and centre, at the heart of the book, forcing us to face the God of the psalms. He has digested a mass of Psalms research and yet releases it in the most palatable and useful doses. I profited immensely from his treatment of the literary design of the Psalter; he helps us see in the Psalms a consciously coherent work (in five books) rather than random bits of poetry. If I were teaching a course on the Psalms, this would be my textbook.'

Dale Ralph Davis

Geoffrey Grogan is a renowned Bible expositor that has worked on major Bible translation projects. He was previously a Principal of Glasgow Bible College (now the International Christian College).

ISBN 1-85792-642-0

Christian Focus Publications

publishes books for all ages
Our mission statement –

STAYING FAITHFUL
In dependence upon God we seek to help make His infallible Word, the Bible, relevant. Our aim is to ensure that the Lord Jesus Christ is presented as the only hope to obtain forgiveness of sin, live a useful life and look forward to heaven with Him.

REACHING OUT
Christ's last command requires us to reach out to our world with His gospel. We seek to help fulfill that by publishing books that point people towards Jesus and help them develop a Christ-like maturity. We aim to equip all levels of readers for life, work, ministry and mission.

Books in our adult range are published in three imprints.

Christian Focus contains popular works including biographies, commentaries, basic doctrine and Christian living. Our children's books are also published in this imprint.

Mentor focuses on books written at a level suitable for Bible College and seminary students, pastors, and other serious readers. The imprint includes commentaries, doctrinal studies, examination of current issues and church history.

Christian Heritage contains classic writings from the past.

Christian Focus Publications, Ltd
Geanies House, Fearn,
Ross-shire, IV20 1TW, Scotland, United Kingdom
info@christianfocus.com

www.christianfocus.com